HOW TO CREATE
TREE SCULPTURE

HOW TO CREATE
TREE SCULPTURE

Step by Step Full Illustrated Instructions

Sal Villano

To order additional copies of this book, contact:
Xlibris Corporation
1-888-795-4274
www.Xlibris.com
Orders@Xlibris.com
28339

CONTENTS

To
Uncle Charlie
For his
Guidance, Encouragement,
and Friendship

I think that I shall never see
A poem lovely as a tree.

A tree whose hungry mouth is prest
Against the earth's sweet flowing breast;

A tree that looks at God all day,
And lifts her leafy arms to pray;

A tree that may in Summer wear
A nest of robins in her hair;

Upon whose bosom snow has lain;
Who intimately lives with rain.

Poems are made by fools like me,
But only God can make a tree.

TREES
by
Joyce Kilmer (1886 - 1918)

BEFORE YOU START

Before you start this or any other art or craft project be sure you keep safety as part of your procedure. Always protect your eyes, lungs and skin with quality made protection devices.

All the material and tools necessary to create any of the three tree sculptures in this book are available from general supply sources, such as: Arts & Craft stores, Hardware stores, Florist supply stores. If you take this book along with you when you are shopping for your supplies you can refer to it and see exactly what is needed. I do not recommend or promote any store, but if you are having trouble obtaining any material or tool described in this book, please contact me and I will be happy to give you the names and addresses of the suppliers I use. I can be contacted at:

> Sal Villano—P.O. Box 514, Miller Place, NY 11764
> Studio Phone & Fax: 631-928-2644
> email: salvillano@gmail.com
> Web Site: www.salvillano.com

I would recommend that you read this entire book before starting. This will help you to understand the next steps before you get to them.

When you are selecting the wire you wish to use to create your tree sculpture, you should keep in mind how wire thickness is gauged. The thickness or "gauge" of the wire is given in numbers. However, THE SMALLER THE NUMBER, THE THICKER THE WIRE. For example:

> *26 gauge wire is THICKER than 28 gauge wire!*

GETTING STARTED

You should also know a little about the type of wire you are using. The wire may change color through the years, but this color change will not affect the strength of the Sculpture. Tree Sculptures that are bonded onto bases using sea sand are for indoor display only. Since the bond is made onto a porous material a water soluble glue is used, therefore the sculptures should never be submerged in water or placed in a dishwasher. Clean and dust your Tree Sculptures with a damp, soft, lint free cloth and use a feather duster for the branches.

WIRE CHARACTERISTICS

WIRE TYPE	CHARACTERISTICS
GOLD	Electroplated onto steel wire to achieve gold color. Insignificant gold content. Will retain gold color for several years, then tarnish or patina. (a patina is a green coating that forms on copper and brass as it ages.)
COPPER	100% copper. Will oxidize slowly and change to a darker copper color, or patina into a dark green color.
SILVER	Electroplated onto steel wire to achieve silver color. Insignificant silver content. Will retain silver color for several years, then tarnish or patina.
RUST	Untreated steel wire. Will rust to a dark brown or dark gray color very quickly.
STEEL	Steel wire galvanized with zinc. Will keep it's flat gray color for many years, then slowly turn darker shades of gray.
BRASS	Will turn a darker brass color and will tarnish and patina.

1. MAKING THE WRAPPING JIG

The word "jig" may be new to you, so I'll explain what it is and what we will use it for. A jig is a devise used to aid, speed up or make more exact the construction or assembly of something else. A jig is used when you wish to create the same thing over and over again to the same standards. The jig itself is not part of the final product, but it is an important part of the process. In this case our jig is used to control the total amount of wire needed for the basic structure of the tree you will be creating. Once you make this jig, save it for future use. It can be altered by changing the position of the nails and the amount of the wire wraps to create larger and different varieties of tree sculptures. It is very simple to construct using a piece of wood (it can be scrap wood) cut to the sizes indicated and three 2 1/2" finishing nails. Finishing nails are the nails without large heads. *fig. 1.*

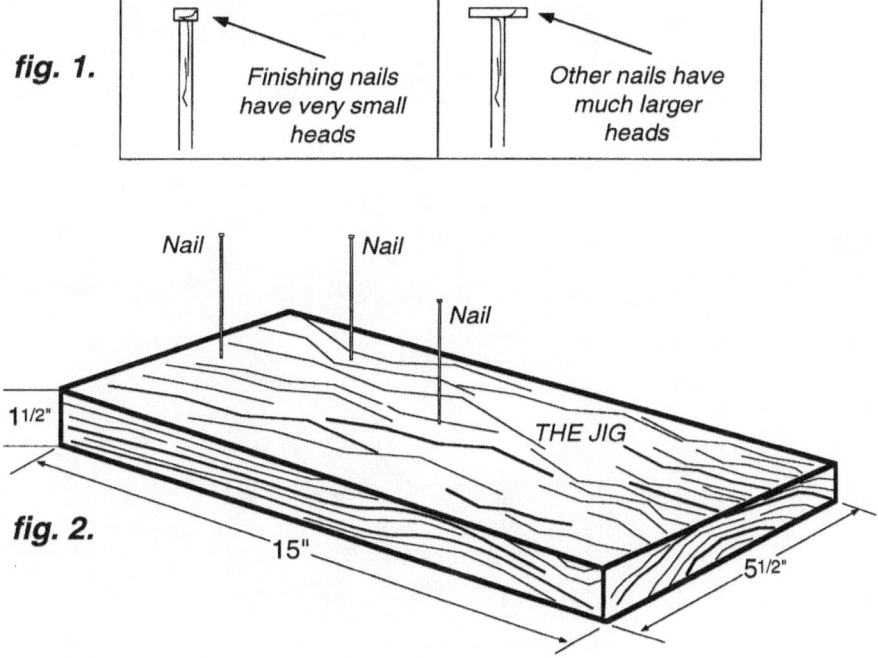

fig. 1.

Finishing Nails — Finishing nails have very small heads

Other Nails — Other nails have much larger heads

Nail Nail Nail

THE JIG

1 1/2"

fig. 2.

15"

5 1/2"

a)

After cutting the wood to the proper size, sand the edges to eliminate any possibility of splinters. *fig 2*. Next, draw pencil lines on the wood to the measurements indicated in *fig. 3* Draw in small dots to indicate where you will position the three finishing nails.

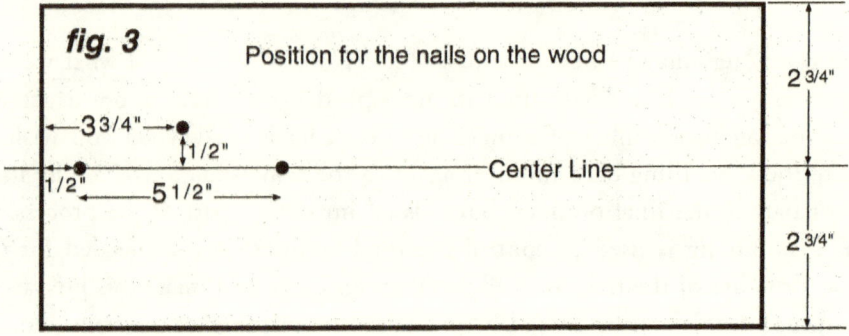

fig. 3   Position for the nails on the wood

b)

Measureth 1/2" up from the point of each of the three finishing nails and mark with pencil. This will indicate how far into the wood you will hammer each nail. *fig. 4.*

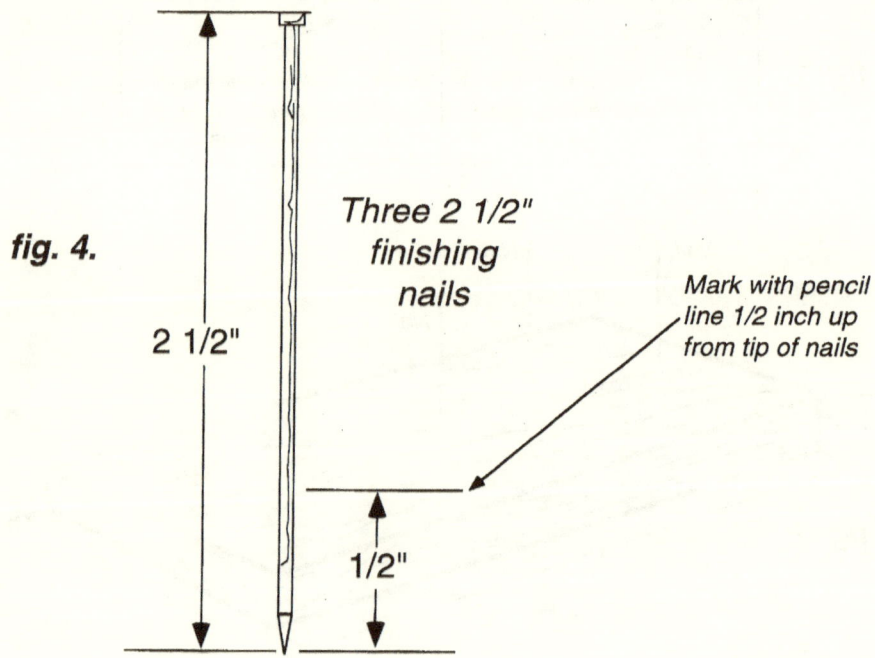

fig. 4.

Three 2 1/2"
finishing
nails

Mark with pencil
line 1/2 inch up
from tip of nails

2 1/2"

1/2"

c)

Hammer the three nails into the wood at the locations you created. Stop driving the nail when it reaches the depth of the pencil line on the tip (1/2"). Be sure the nails are hammered in as straight as possible.

2. WRAPPING THE WIRE

a)

Create a small loop around any of the nails you hammered into the jig. *fig. 5*. This loop will anchor the wire so it does not come off while you are wrapping the rest of the wire for the tree. Work directly from your wire source. Do not try to hold the wire source in your hand while you are wrapping. Unwrap about 3 feet of wire before you start. This will make the wrapping process much easier. You may find in the course of wrapping the wire for this step or upcoming steps that the wire may sometimes get tangled or twisted. If this should happen, stop wrapping and twirl the wire in the opposite direction to remove any kinks.

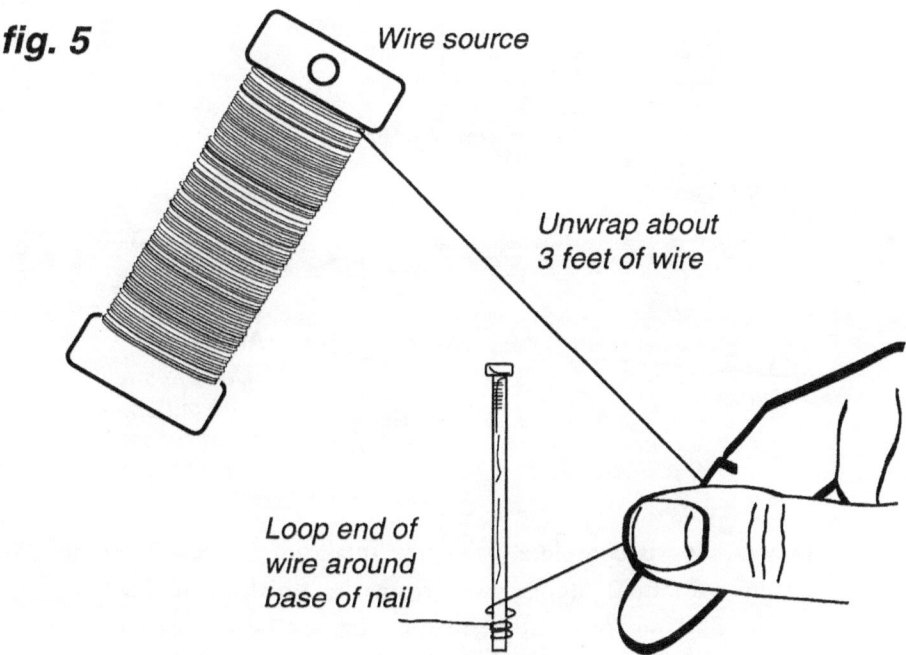

fig. 5

Wire source

Unwrap about 3 feet of wire

Loop end of wire around base of nail

b)

Wrap the wire 35 times around the outside of all three of the finishing nails that are in the jig. *fig. 6.* Do not wrap the wire too tightly. You will have to slip the wire off the nails when you are finished wrapping. One wrap is completed when you are back at the point from which you started the wrapping. It does not matter where you start the wrapping, or in which direction you proceed, but be sure to keep count and end at 35 wraps. While you are wrapping keep the wire bundle close to the base of the nails, this will help to prevent the wire from slipping off the nails. If you find that any of the nails are working loose while you are wrapping, this is an indication that you are wrapping the wire too tight. If this should happen, unwrap the wire bundle back onto the wire source, hammer in the nails a little deeper, and start again to wrap the wire.

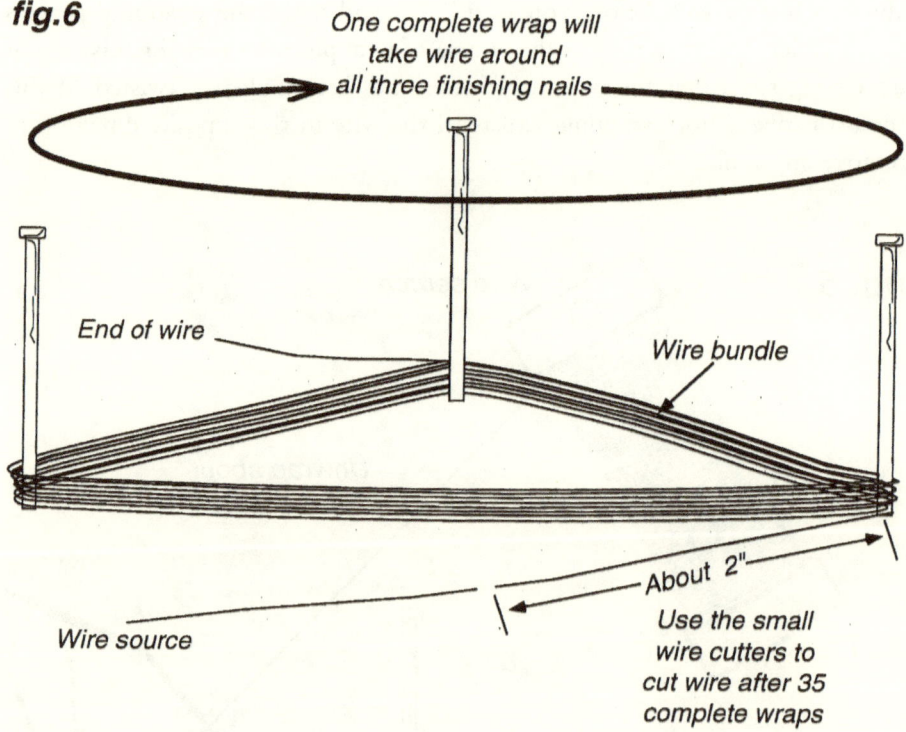

fig.6

One complete wrap will take wire around all three finishing nails

End of wire

Wire bundle

About 2"

Wire source

Use the small wire cutters to cut wire after 35 complete wraps

c)

When the wrapping is complete, using the small wire cutters, carefully cut the wire source about 2 inches away from the finishing nail where you completed the 35th wrap. Gently slip the wrapped bundle of wire off the finishing nails. The wire bundle should look like a triangle with a straight wire at one end and a coiled wire at the other end. Uncoil the small section of wire that was used to hold the wire on the nail and straighten it out. *fig. 7.*

This completes the need for the jig. You can put it away, however, you may want to use it again to create other tree sculptures.

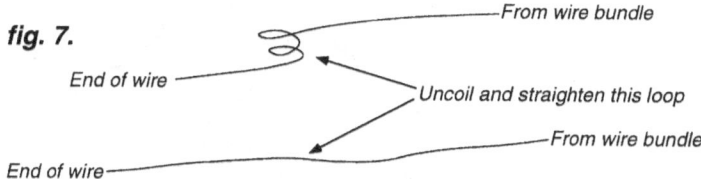

fig. 7.

End of wire

From wire bundle

Uncoil and straighten this loop

From wire bundle

End of wire

d)
Hold the completed wire bundle in both hands and shape the bundle into an oval. *fig 8.* Try to unbend, as much as possible, the corners of the bundle that were shaped by being wrapped around the nails. Leave both ends of the wire extended out of the bundle. One end of the wire should be about 2" long.

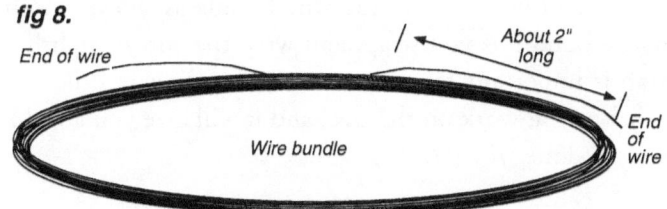

fig 8.

End of wire

About 2" long

Wire bundle

End of wire

e)
Firmly hold the wire bundle about 1/3 the distance in from the curve at the end of the bundle. *fig 9.*

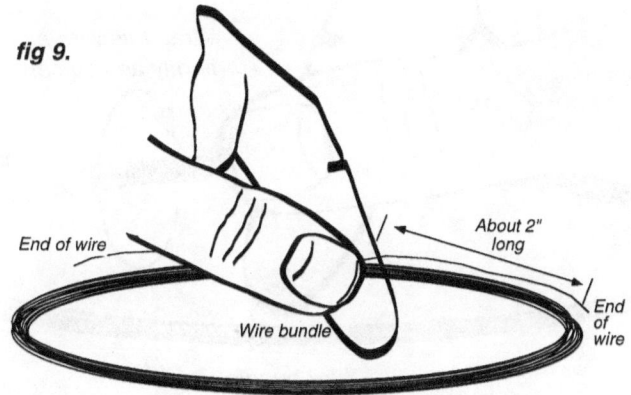

fig 9.

End of wire

About 2" long

Wire bundle

End of wire

f)

While holding the wire bundle firmly in one hand, use your other hand to bend up the end piece of wire. The section of wire you bent up is be about 2″ long. *fig. 10.*

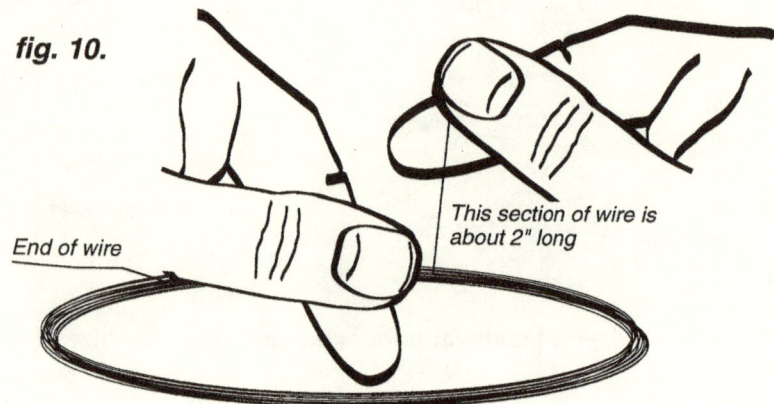

fig. 10.

End of wire

This section of wire is about 2″ long

g)

Wrap the 2″ piece of wire around the wire bundle as shown. Keep your firm grip on the wire bundle as you wrap, and wrap the wire as tightly as you can. The first wrap is important for two reasons. It is the wrap that will hold the bundle together as you work on the tree, and it will give you a feel for how the wire wrapping is done. *fig. 11.*

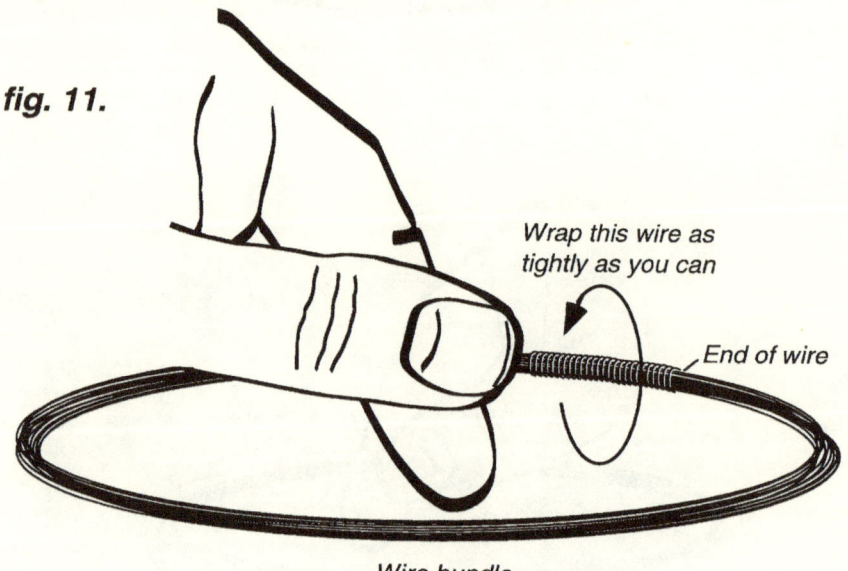

fig. 11.

Wrap this wire as tightly as you can

End of wire

Wire bundle

h)

Using the medium wire cutters, cut through the entire wire bundle about 1" from the curve. This may take a few cuts, but be sure the wire bundle is cut all the way through. *fig. 12.*

fig. 12.

Be sure to cut all the wires

Wire coil

Wire bundle

j)

After all the wire in the bundle is cut, unbend both curves in the bundle *fig. 13* so you are left with one straight bundle of wire held together by the end wire wrapping.

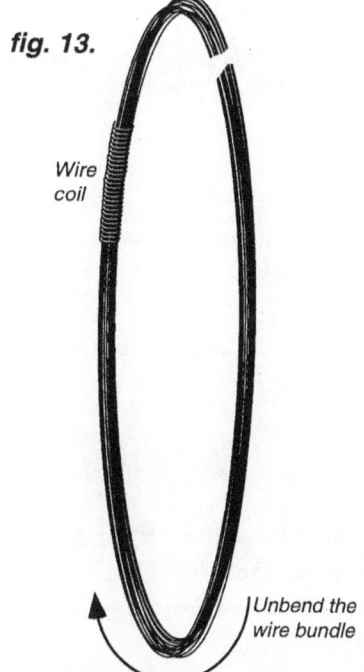

fig. 13.

Wire coil

Unbend the wire bundle

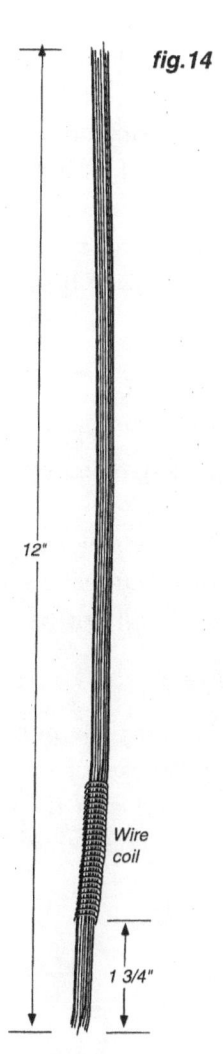

fig.14

12"

Wire coil

1 3/4"

k)

At this point the structure should look like *fig. 14.* The measurements do not have to be exactly as stated, but should be close.

3. CREATING THE ROOT SYSTEM

The roots of trees are very interesting. As with all elements in nature, each tree has a unique character all its own. Some trees have deep roots that can not be seen from the surface, with most of the root system buried deep into the earth. Other trees have roots that appear to be only on the surface of the earth and offer an exciting view of how they support the rest of the tree. It is the trees that offer us this view that I find most interesting.

When creating the roots of your tree do not try to follow exactly what is shown here. Use the technique as a guide as you create a root system that is yours. Do not be concerned about counting the wraps or if your coiling is not too tight. If the roots you create are a little larger or smaller than shown here, it is really not that important to the final outcome. The result you should be aware of, is if the roots appear to be supporting the tree. When you look at your roots and they look like they are solid, stable and strong, you have created an effective root system. The roots I will show you how to create will be partially buried in the root mound to help support your tree, therefore it is better to create them larger, rather than smaller.

I have found in my own observations of the root system of most trees, that they are usually growing in odd numbers and at very interesting angles, with non symmetrical twists and turns.

You are now ready to start wrapping and creating the roots and the rest of the tree. You will be working from the same wire source for the entire tree. This wire will not be cut until the tree is completely finished.

a)
Holding the bundle firmly in the area where the wire coil is, separate the lower part of roots into three approximately equal sections. *fig. 15.* Don't be concerned if the three parts are not exactly equal. The root system will look more interesting if the roots are of different size and shape.

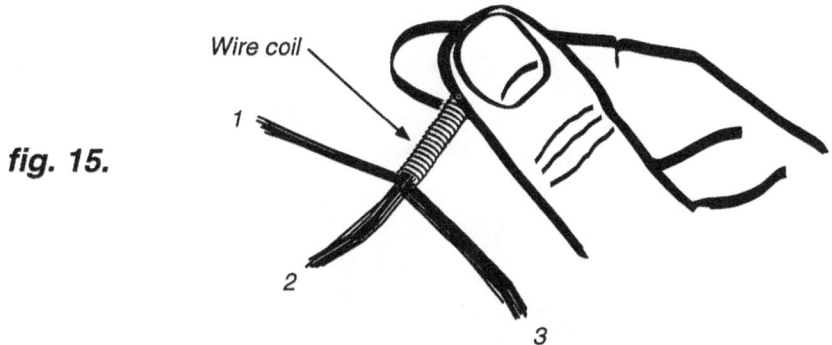

fig. 15.

b)

You are now going to start to wrap the rest of the tree. Using your wire source, wrap wire tightly up the wire coil toward the top of the tree. *fig. 16.* This first wiring is used to anchor the wire, so you only need enough to hold the rest of the wire in place as you wrap. This wire will eventually be wired over when you add thickness to the tree trunk.

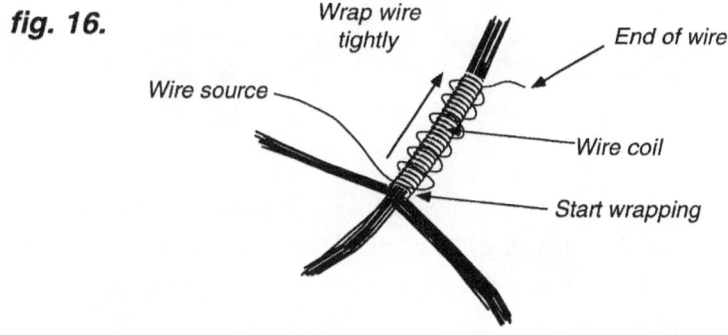

fig. 16.

c)

Using your wire source, start circular wrapping one of the root sections from the base of the trunk out toward the end of the root. You can start this wrapping with any root section. Wrap the source wire half way down the root section, then stop. At the point where you stopped wrapping the source wire, separate the remaining root section into 2 more approximately equal root group sections. Loop the wire through the "V" section of the root, then back to the base of the trunk. *fig. 17.* d) Repeat step c) for 1 more root section. The final root section will not be divided in 2. It will be left as one large root to create a more interesting root system.

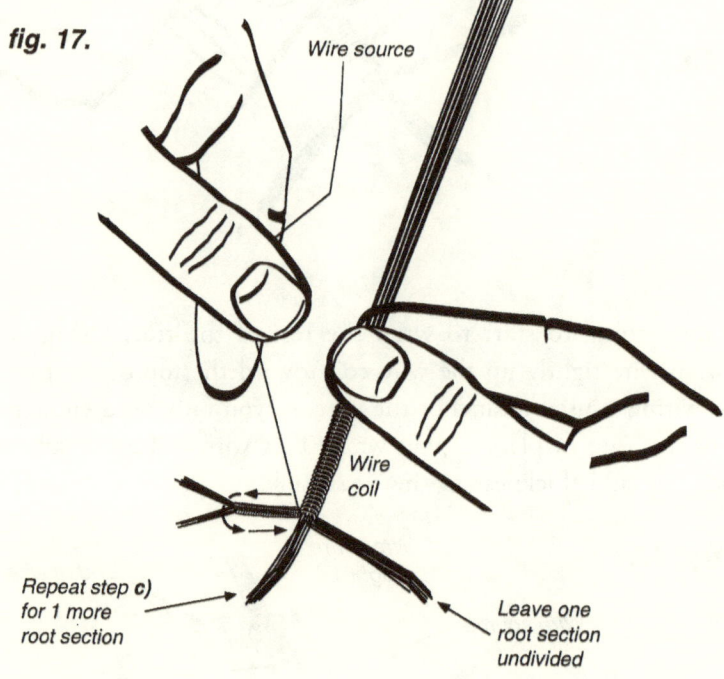

fig. 17.

Wire source

Wire coil

Repeat step *c)* for 1 more root section

Leave one root section undivided

e)

Separate and fan out all the individual root wires of the final root section. *fig. 18.* This is the section you did not divide into 2 parts. It will be the largest root section. This root section was created to be different than the other two in order to add variety and interest to the root system.

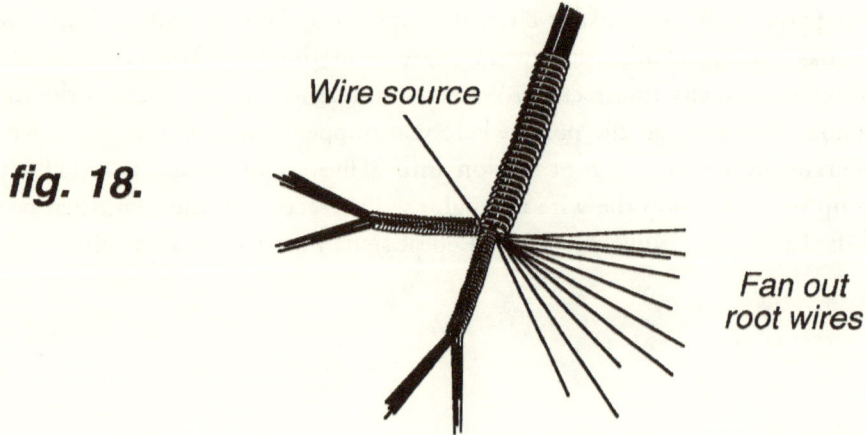

Wire source

fig. 18.

Fan out root wires

f)

Starting with the longest root wire, using the small wire clippers, snip off the ends of each strand of wire progressively but only slightly smaller than the one before. *fig. 19.* Before you start this step look carefully at the location where you will make the cuts. Remember, if you cut any root section too short, it will not grow back!

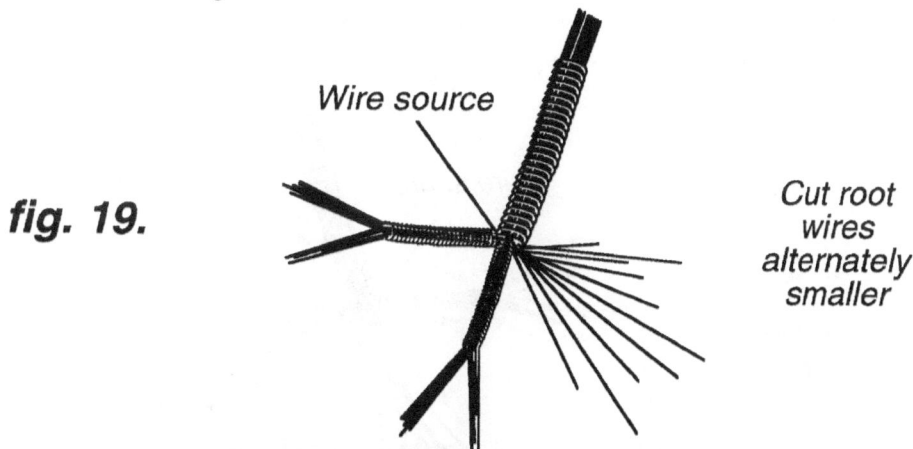

Wire source

fig. 19.

Cut root wires alternately smaller

g)

Repeat the fanning and snipping procedure as described in steps e) & f) for the 2 other smaller root sections.

h)

Working with 1 root section at a time, squeeze the root wires together to create a total of 5 separate root points. Because you cut the ends of each root wire to several different sizes, the root ends will be tapered. This taper will give the wire root a more realistic look. *fig. 20.*

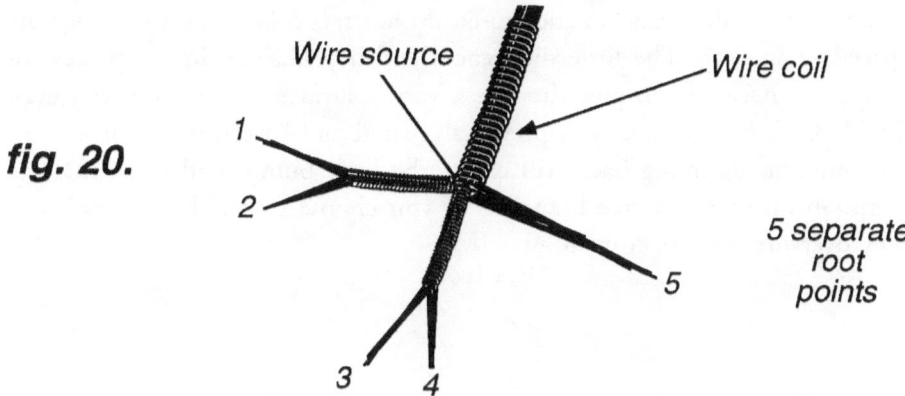

Wire source

Wire coil

fig. 20.

1

2

5 separate root points

5

3   4

i)

Using the wire source, slowly wrap the wire on to each root section. Wrap the wire to the end of each root then back to the trunk then on to the next root. *fig. 21.* You should end up with the wire source at the bottom of the trunk, where all the roots meet. When wrapping wire around the roots and all parts of the tree, do not try to keep the wire equally spaced from the wrap before. Let the wire create irregular shapes and little bumps. This technique when will create a far more interesting surface texture for your tree.

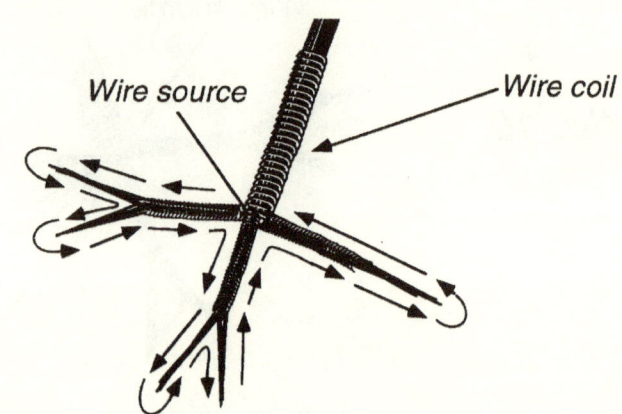

fig. 21.

4. WIRING THE TRUNK & BRANCHES

Wiring the trunk and branches requires the same basic technique as was used to wire the roots, except now there is much more wiring, and over wiring involved. You should by now be fairly proficient in the process of wiring the tree. If you feel you are not proficient, you will be very soon! Once again, as you are wiring the branches and trunk, do not try to keep the wiring equally spaced or smooth. The little differences and irregularities in the process of wiring are necessary to give the tree a varied surface texture. You can even double back over an area you previously wired and "overwire" it for a small section. This doubling back will create the little bumps and stubs that are common on so many tree branches. If you choose to try this "overwiring" only overwire for 3 or 4 wraps.

a)

Separate the top section of the tree into 2 equal parts. *fig. 22.* Start the separation at the top of the trunk coil wrap.

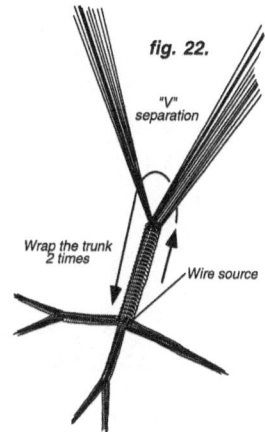

fig. 22.

"V" separation

b)

Wrap the wire source up to the "V" separation in the branches pass it through the "V" then back down the trunk. Repeat this wrap 2 times to create a thicker trunk. End the wrapping at the base of the trunk. *fig. 22.*

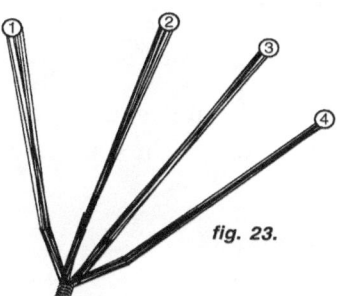

Wrap the trunk 2 times

Wire source

c)

Separate the 2 main branches into 2 more equal parts. Creating a total of 4 branches. *fig. 23.*

fig. 23.

d)

Wrap the wire source up the trunk and onto any one of the 4 branches. Stop this wrap about 1 inch up the branch. Separate the wires of this branch into 2 parts. Pass the wire through the "V" then back down to the top of the trunk. Continue down, and repeat this procedure for the remaining branches. *fig. 24.* You will have created a total of 8 branches when this step is completed.

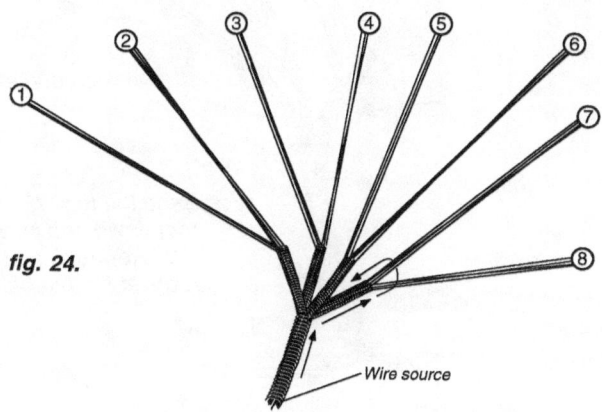

fig. 24.

Wire source

5. FORMING THE TREE

a) Use fig. 26. for: a), b), c), & d).
Spread out the 3 root sections of the tree to form a tripod. Even though the tree is still thin, it should be able to stand on this base you created.

b)
Twist 2 of the branches together at their base to form one larger branch with 2 smaller branches growing out of it.

c)
Bend the tops of all three root sections in toward the trunk.

d)
Bend all three roots at irregular angles, none of the roots should be straight. Also give a slight bend to the trunk.

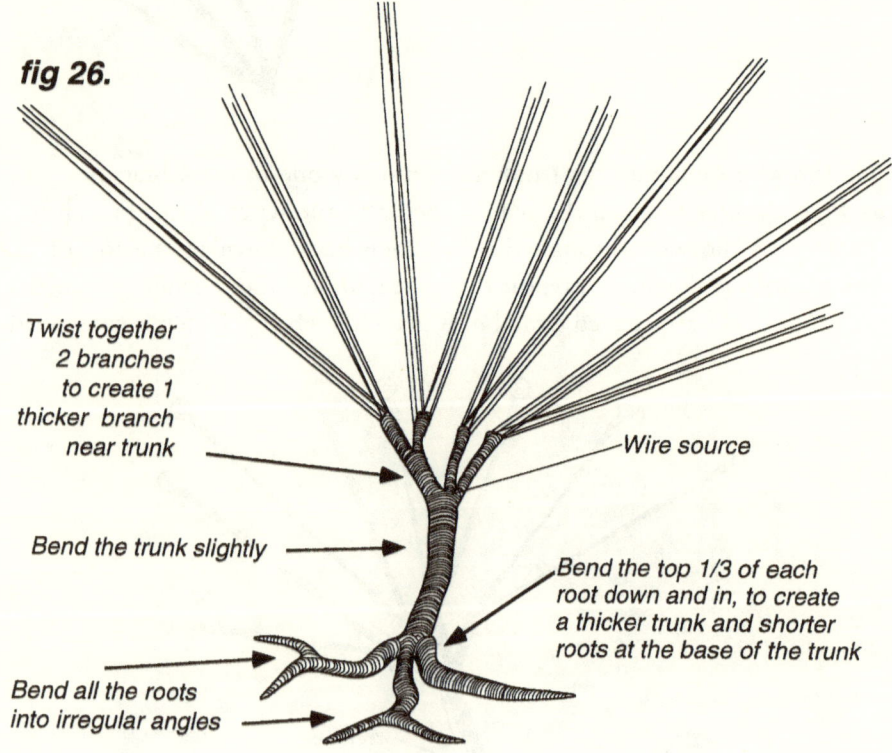

fig 26.

Twist together
2 branches
to create 1
thicker branch
near trunk

Wire source

Bend the trunk slightly

Bend the top 1/3 of each
root down and in, to create
a thicker trunk and shorter
roots at the base of the trunk

Bend all the roots
into irregular angles

e)

Wrap the wire source down the trunk and onto each root section. Do not wrap the wire to the tip of each root, but stop the wrap and return when you are half way toward the tip. Wrap all the tops of the root sections that are at the very bottom of the trunk as if they were part of the trunk. This will create a trunk with a very thick and interesting base. End wrapping at the top of the trunk. *fig. 27.*

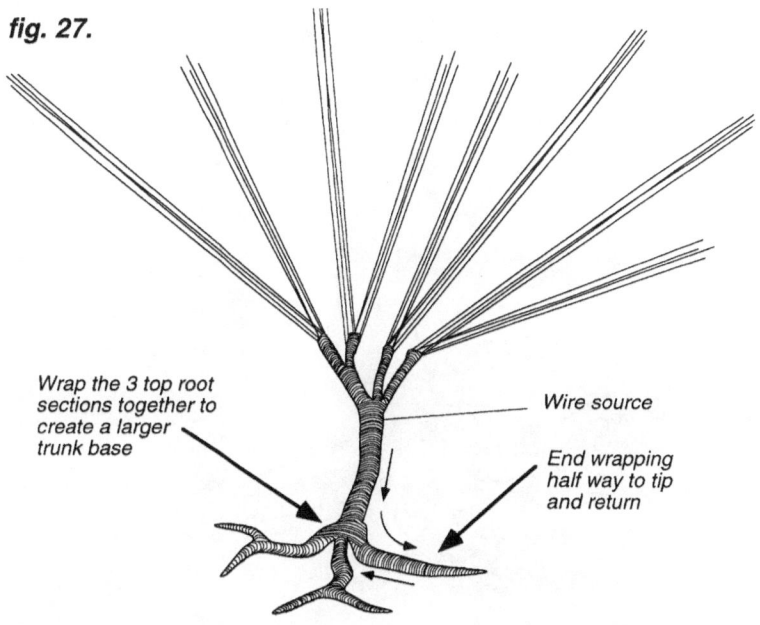

fig. 27.

Wrap the 3 top root sections together to create a larger trunk base

Wire source

End wrapping half way to tip and return

6. THICKENING THE TREE

a)

Continue wrapping the tree to thicken the trunk and roots. Once again, do not wrap the wire all the way to the end of the roots, but stop and return at different points along the way. *fig. 27.*

b)

Wrap the base of the trunk and the area where the roots enter the trunk several more time so they are thicket in these areas. Do not keep count of the number of times you wrap. I ask for "several" wraps just to give you an idea about how many to do. *fig. 28.*

c)

Apply the same procedure for the branches as you did for the roots. However, this time wire all the way to the end of the thicker branch coil, then return. Repeat this wrapping process for all the branches. *fig. 28.*

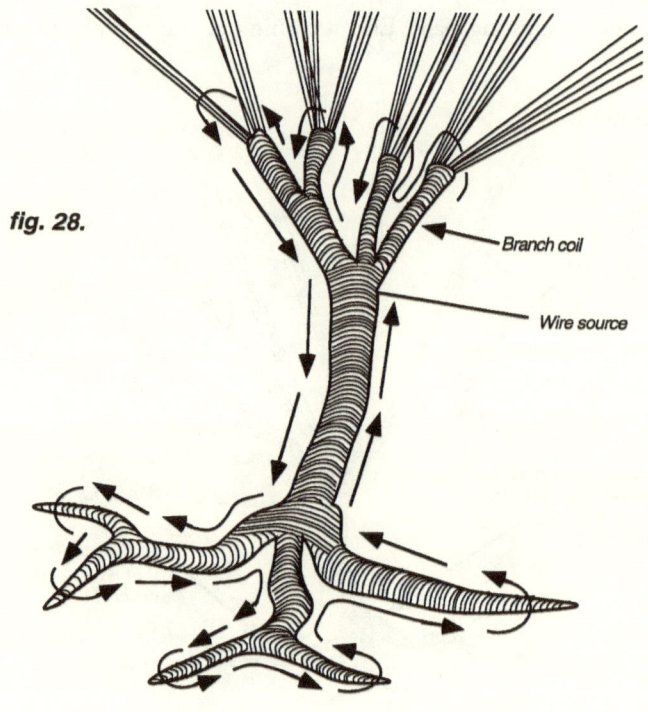

fig. 28.

Branch coil

Wire source

7. FINAL BRANCHING

a) Use *fig. 29.* for: a), b), & c).

Separate the remaining wire of each branch into 2 approximately equal amounts. You will find that some of the remaining branches will have even amounts and some will have odd amounts. This is not a problem and will be worked out in later steps.

b)

Tightly twist each separate group of wire together to create an entirely new branch. Twist the wire until the new branch is about 3/4" to 1" long. You should now have about 16 total branches in your tree.

c)
The final branch sections are not wrapped with wire. The surface texture for these branches is created simply by twisting the wire. The tighter you twist these final wires, the more irregularities your tree branches will have.

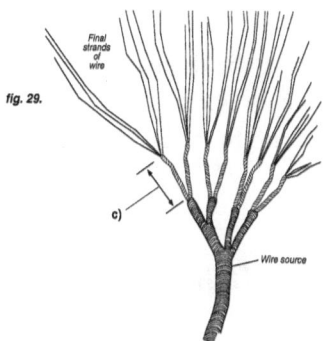

fig. 29.

8. CREATING THE ROOT ANCHORS

The final use for the wire source is to create an anchor that will hold the tree into the base material. This anchor will not be seen when the tree is completed.

a)
Wrap the wire source down the trunk and half way out onto any root. Create a double wire loop about 1 1/2" long. Proceed back up the root, and down onto any other root. Create the same type of double loop on this root. Cut the wire source after completing the second loop. *fig. 30.*

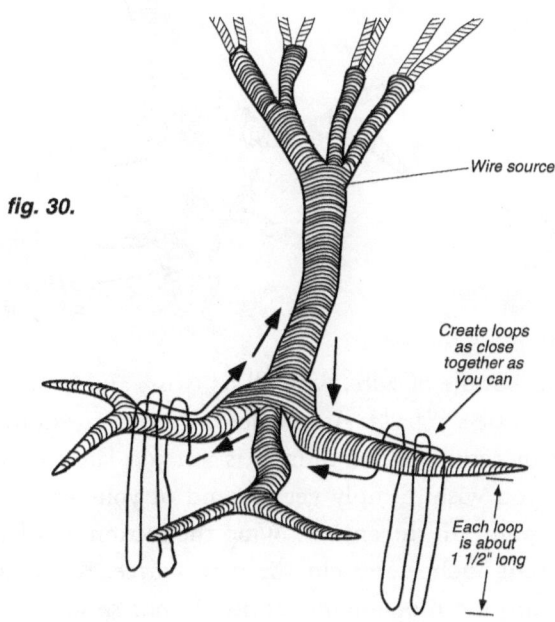

fig. 30.

Wire source

Create loops as close together as you can

Each loop is about 1 1/2" long

b)

Twist the double loops to create one thick loop. Repeat this for the other root anchor wires. Twist the wire tightly so it is wrapped tightly against the bottom of the root. *fig. 31.*

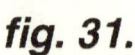
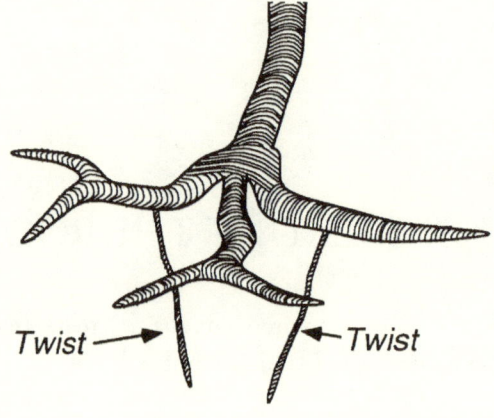

fig. 31.

Twist ⟶   ⟵ Twist

c)

Twist both double anchor wires together about half way up their distances. This will create one large anchor that will be bonded into the sand and the glue to hold the tree firmly in place. *fig. 32.*

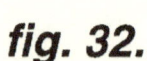
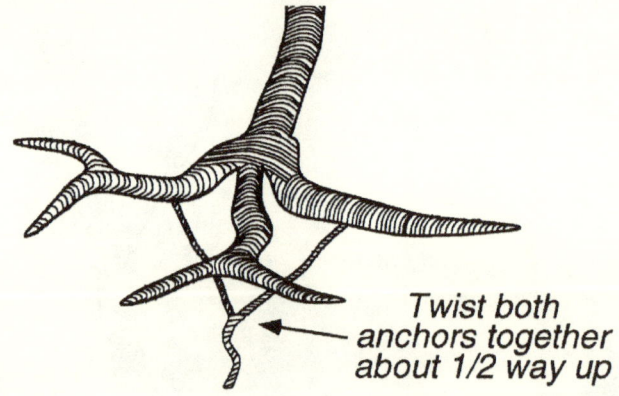

fig. 32.

Twist both anchors together about 1/2 way up

At this stage your bundle of wire, with all its twists and bends should actually start to look like a tree. *fig. 33.* As you look at your creation, if you feel the trunk, branches or roots are too thin, it is not too late to go back and add thickness where you wish. Simply get the end of your wire source and start wrapping at any point on the anchor. Wrap the section you feel needs it, end up back at the root anchor and cut the wire source. Remember the anchor will be bonded into the root mound, so it will not show.

fig. 33.

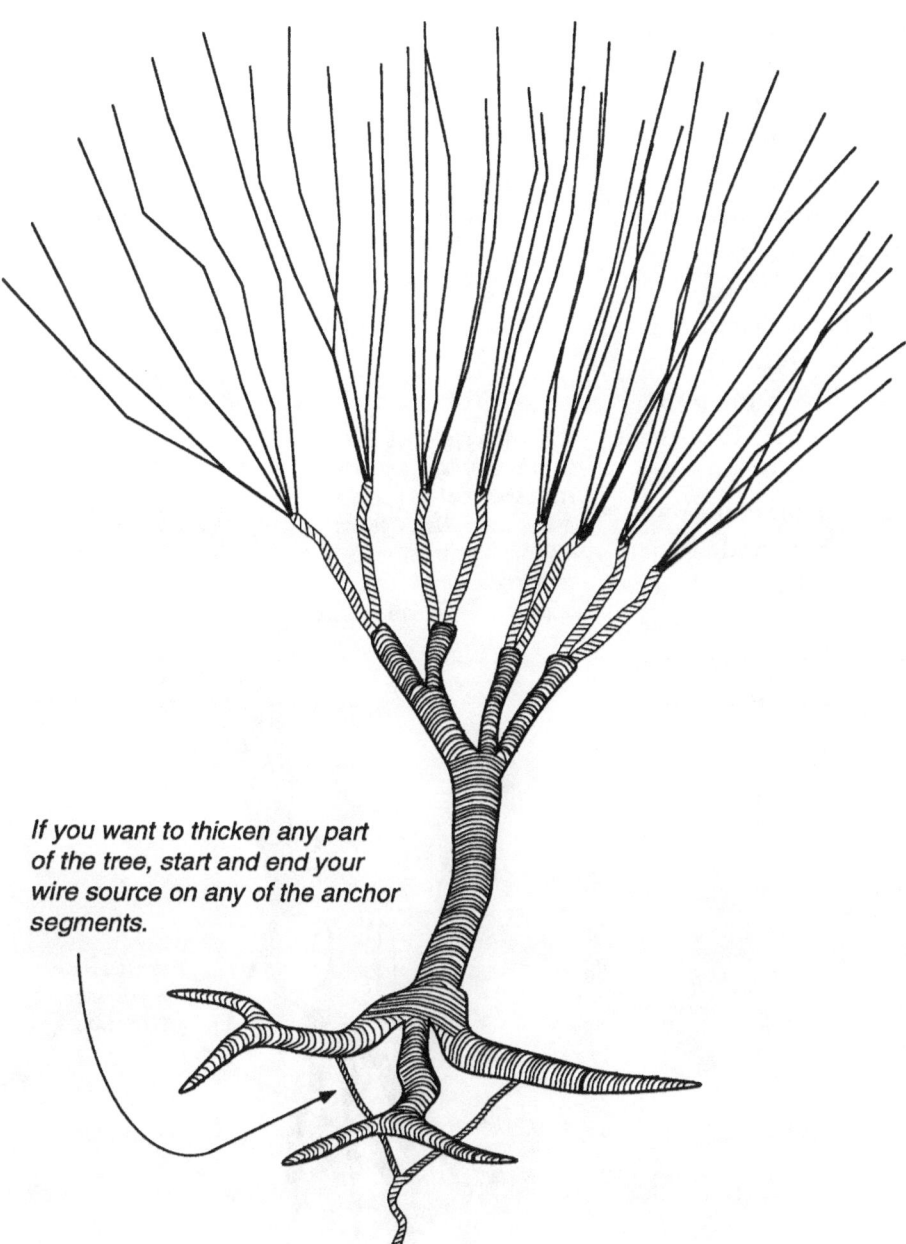

If you want to thicken any part of the tree, start and end your wire source on any of the anchor segments.

9. PREPARING THE TREE FOR MOUNTING

a) Hold the tree firmly by the trunk and gather all of the branches together and point them up. This will keep the branches out of the way as you proceed. *fig. 34.*

b) Still holding the tree firmly, gather the roots together and point them down. Tuck the anchor wires into the center of the roots. Your tree is now ready to be mounted on its base, place it aside for now as we prepare the base and the root mound. *fig. 34.*

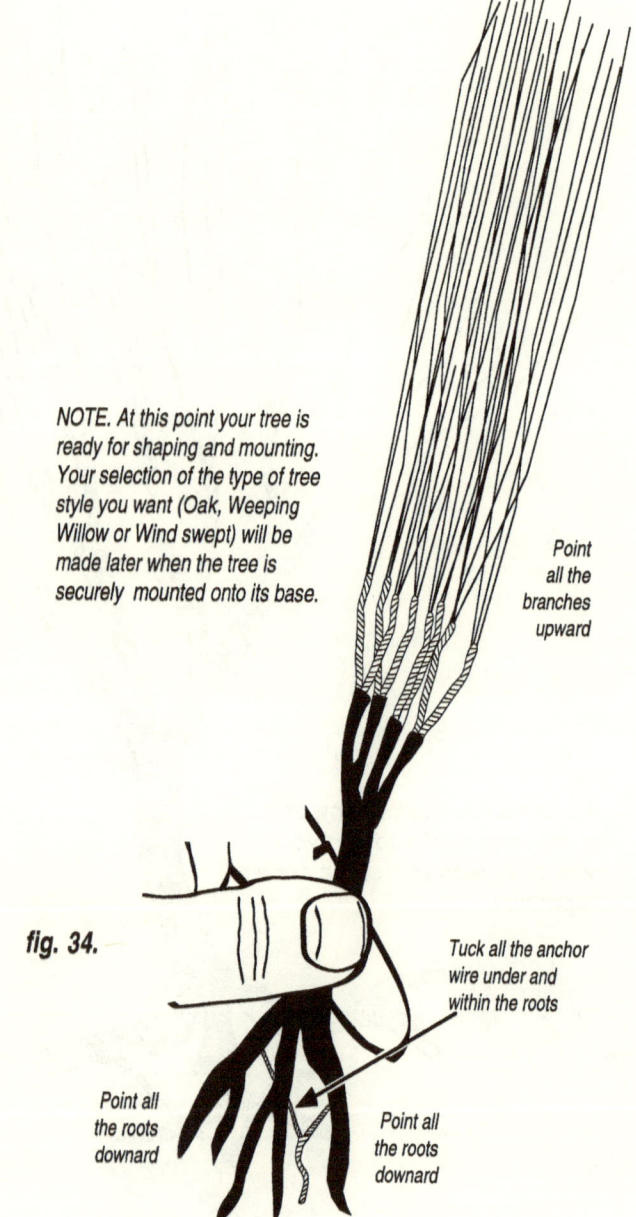

NOTE. At this point your tree is ready for shaping and mounting. Your selection of the type of tree style you want (Oak, Weeping Willow or Wind swept) will be made later when the tree is securely mounted onto its base.

Point all the branches upward

fig. 34.

Tuck all the anchor wire under and within the roots

Point all the roots downard

Point all the roots downard

10. PREPARING THE BASE FOR THE TREE

You can use any porous surface as a base on which to mount the tree, such as rocks, pottery, wood, glass, etc. Just be sure the base you select is compatible with the white glue you will be using. Read the label on the glue package and it will inform you as to the surfaces that the glue will stick to. The shape and style of the tree has not yet been created. You will do this when the tree is permanently mounted on its base. When selecting the size of the base be sure it does not overpower the size of the tree. The mass of the base should be optically only a little bigger then the tree itself. After you have created the tree in its base and if you feel the size is not correct, you can place the base and the tree in clean water for a few hours, and the white glue in the base will dissolve and free the tree. After you dry the tree, you can try again. For this tree I have selected a piece of dark green free formed glass, that I purchased in an art and craft store. This is the type of base that is shown on the cover of this book.

a)

Place a piece of double stick tape or fold over a piece of masking tape onto the bottom of your base. Use enough tape to hold the base securely. The tape will hold the base in position in the tray as you work on creating the sand mound. The mound will hold the tree erect. *fig. 35.*

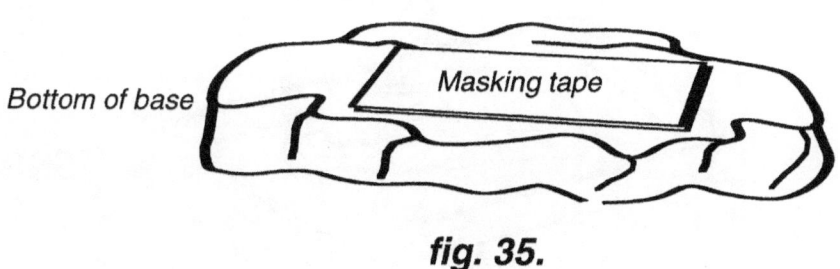

Bottom of base   Masking tape

fig. 35.

b)

Place the base, tape side down, in the center of the tray or saucer. Press the base firmly onto the tray to be sure the tape is holding. *fig. 36.* The base will stay in this tray for the entire process of creating the root mound.

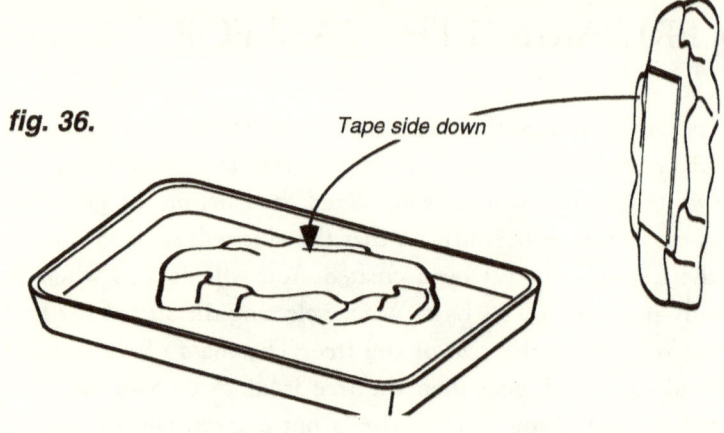

fig. 36.

Tape side down

c)

Put 4 to 5 drops of the white glue onto the center of the base. Be careful not to get any glue on the tray (we don't want to glue the base to the tray!) If you find the glue running over the sides, wipe it clean and start again. This glue spot will be the first anchor for the root mound. *fig. 37.*

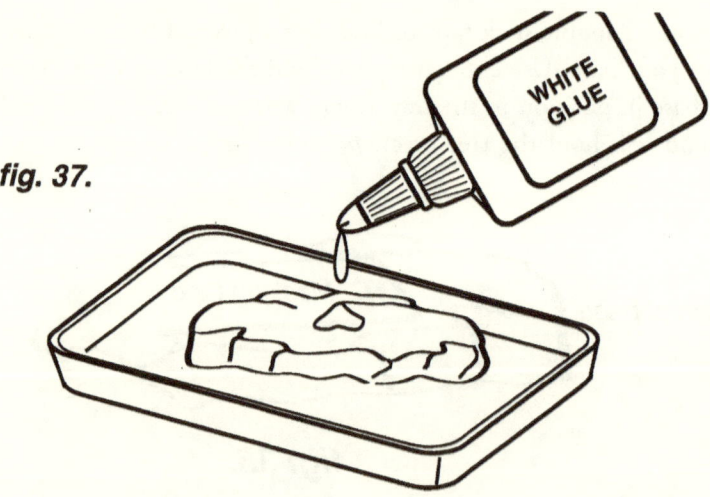

fig. 37.

WHITE GLUE

d)

Sprinkle on enough sand to cover the entire glue spot. I like to use an old spoon, but you can just sprinkle it on by hand if you like. Don't be concerned about putting on too much sand. The glue spot will only absorb as much as it can hold and the rest of the sand will remain loose. Let this mixture dry overnight. *fig 38.* From this point on, the glue and sand mixture will be called the root mound.

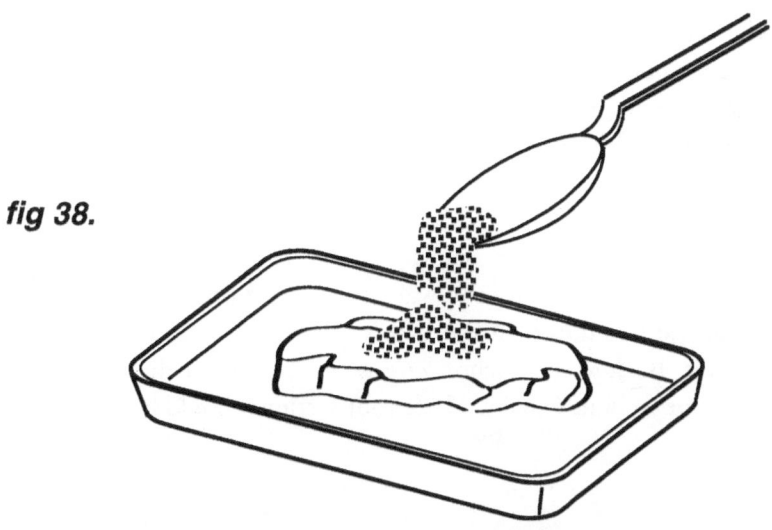

fig 38.

e)
After the glue and sand is dry, I recomend you let it dry overnight. Use the soft brush to remove the excess sand from the top of your base. Simply brush the sand into the tray. *fig. 39.*

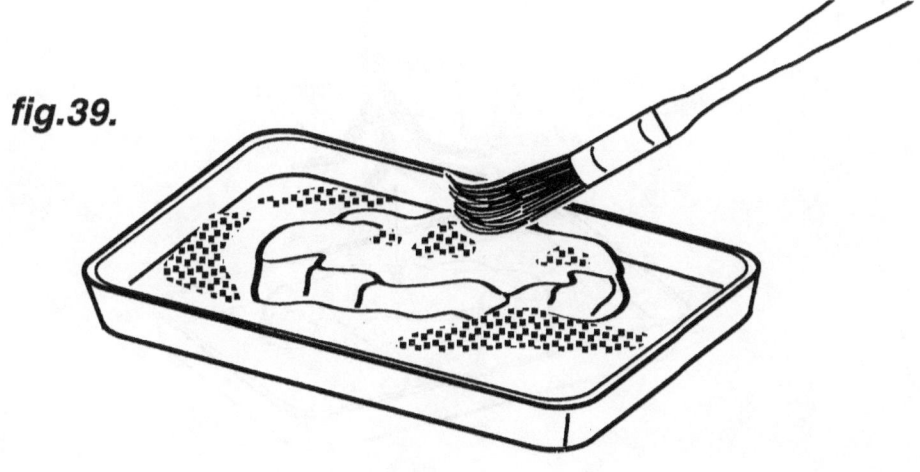

fig.39.

11. MOUNTING THE TREE ONTO THE BASE

The tree will be bound to the base in several steps. The first few steps will bond the tree to the root mound and the remaining steps will create an interesting support structure from which the roots will appear to be growing. Once again, each time you apply a layer of the glue and sand mixture it should be thoroughly dried before the next layer is applied.

a)
Spread the three root sections slightly apart. At about the half way point of each root section bend the root upward so it will support the tree. Gently but firmly push the tree down on the base so the three main root sections begin to spread out. Be sure the anchor wire is tucked within the root area. Try to spread the root sections equally. These root sections should be optically spaced. *fig. 40.*

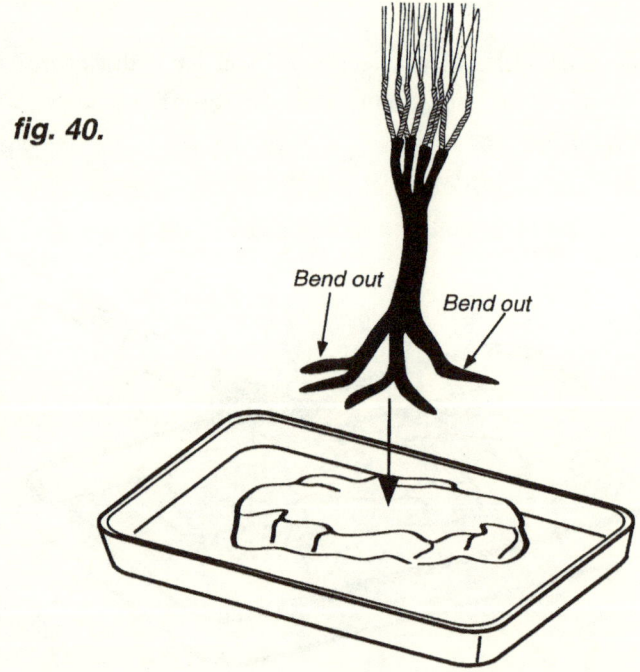

fig. 40.

Bend out

Bend out

b)
After the roots are spread out, the tree will be able to stand erect on the base. Using the masking tape, tape the tree to the tray. Tape only the bottom of the

tree. *fig. 41*. This taping step is only a temporary hold until we secure the entire tree firmly to the tray.

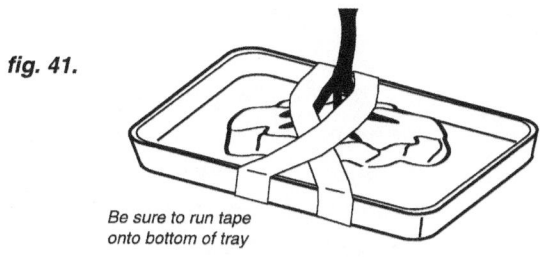

fig. 41.

Be sure to run tape
onto bottom of tray

c)
Gently hold the tree by the trunk and divide the branches into 2 equal groups. Fold the branches over and tape them to the sides and the bottom of the tray. This is the taping step that will hold the tree in place for the rest of the gluing procedure. Be sure the branches are securely fastened to the tray, use plenty of tape. *fig. 42*.

d)
When tree is securely fastened to the tray by its branches you can remove the tape that is on the roots.

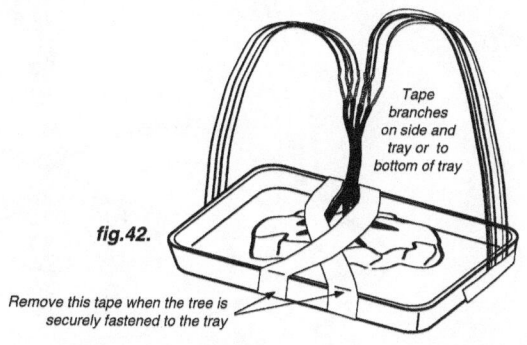

Tape
branches
on side and
tray or to
bottom of tray

fig.42.

Remove this tape when the tree is
securely fastened to the tray

12. CREATING THE ROOT MOUND

The root mound is very important to the overall appearance of the tree sculpture. The main purpose of the root mound is of course to hold the tree onto the base. The visual purpose of the root mound is to make it appear as if the tree is actually growing out of the center of the mound. To these ends, It is far better to have less root mound rather than more. The roots of the tree will look much more realistic if they are only slightly imbedded in the mound, not covered by it. The top 1/3 of each root, as a minimum, should be visible.

To insure the strength of the root mound, it is important that each layer of
the sand and glue mixture is completely dry and solid, before you start the
next step.

a)
Construct a "sand dam" around the entire base of the trees root system. The
tips of the roots should be buried in the sand, but the center of the tree
directly under the trunk must be empty. This is the void you will fill with the
glue and sand mixture to hold the tree in place. You should still be able to see
the original glue mound when you look between the roots. *fig. 43*. If you find
you have put in too much sand, dump all the sand and create a new sand
dam.

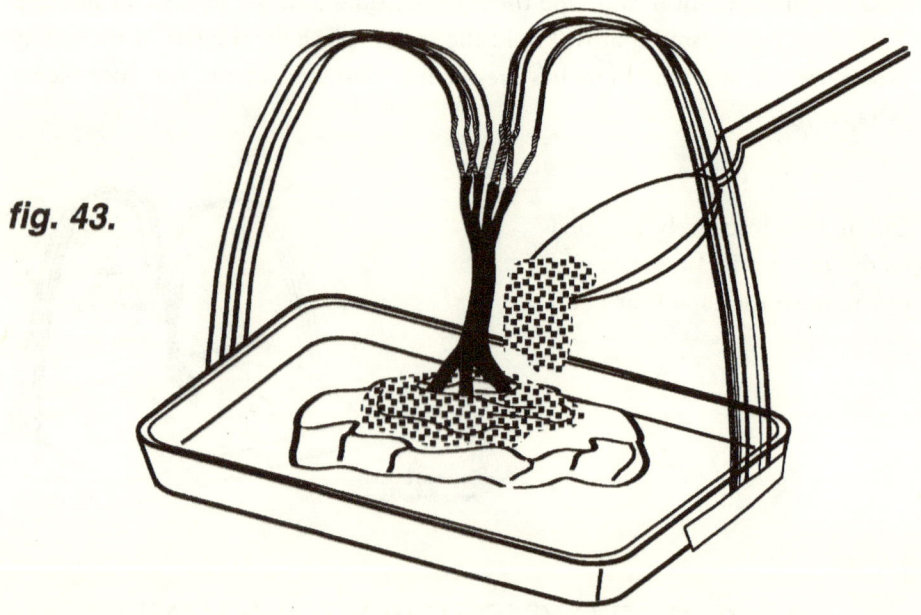

fig. 43.

b)
Apply about 25 to 30 drops of the white glue directly into the center of the
sand dam. *fig. 44*. Be careful not to put in too much glue. The sand dam will
hold the glue in place for the next step. The total amount of glue should fill
the void in the center only about half way. Proceed slowly during this step, it
is much better to put in too little glue rather than too much. Remember, this

root mound will be created in layers, so you can easily add more layers later on. Be sure that the glue is flowing in and around the root anchor.

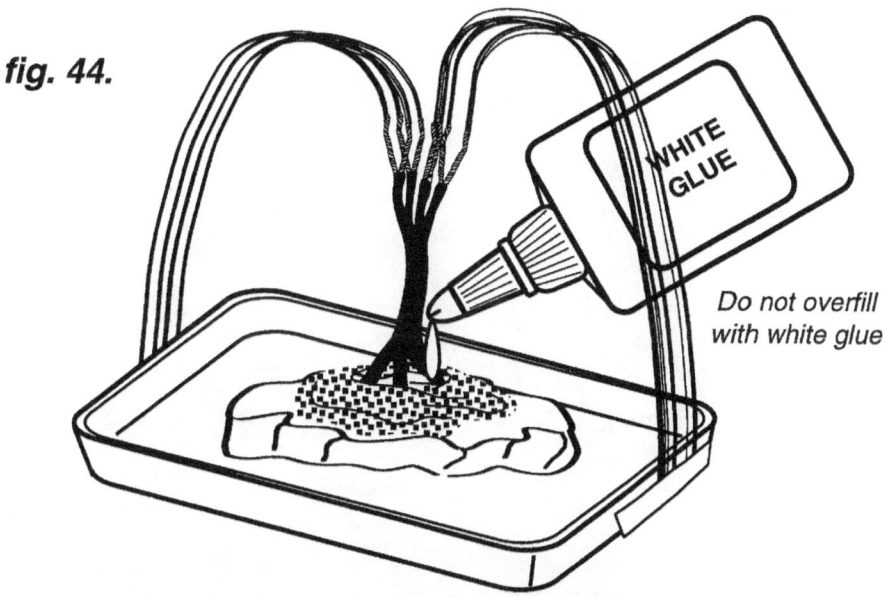

fig. 44.

WHITE GLUE

Do not overfill with white glue

c)
Slowly add more sand to the rim of the sand dam until it is completely covered. Add the sand from the outer edge toward the center of the tree as you proceed around. Add the sand slowly and only a little at a time. Do not move the tree or the tray as you are adding the sand. When you are finished adding the sand, you should not be able to see any of the root structure. *fig. 45*. Let this dry overnight.

d)
After you are sure the sand mound is completely dry, brush away all the loose sand from around the roots and inside the root area. Since the tree is securely fastened to the tray, you can dump the sand from the tray as you hold on to the tree and tray together.

e)
Build another sand dam as you did before. This time construct the dam so that when you fill it with the glue and sand mixture it will reach up to the bottom of the trunk area. Again, if you find you have used too much sand for the dam, dump it and start again.

f)

For this layer, add about 5 to 10 drops of glue into the center and once again cover the entire sand dam with sand, and let it dry overnight.

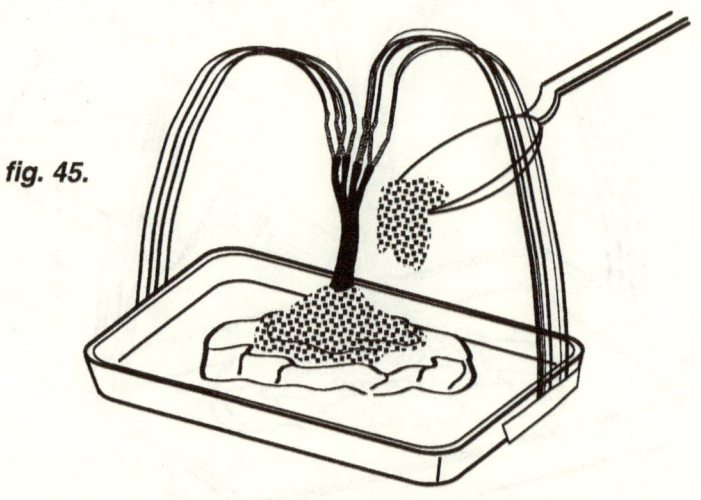

fig. 45.

13. FINAL CONSTRUCTION OF
THE ROOT MOUND

a)

When you are sure the sand dam is completely dry and is hard to the touch, brush away all the loose sand then dump any excess sand out of the tray. Since this sand has no glue on it, you can save it and use it for additional tree sculpture.

b)

If you see any voids or spaces in the root mound that you would like to fill in, place 1 or 2 drops of the white glue in the void, then add the sand and cover the area as you did before. If any of the voids are large enough to require more than 1 or 2 drops of glue, fill these in a layer at a time. As a alternative to filling any voids with just sand, you can also place small pebbles in the void and glue them in. Just put 1 or 2 drops of glue in the void, add the pebble into the glue, then cover it all with sand. I find the root systems look more interesting and realistic if they have less sand and glue, rather than more. The root mound should look like it can easily support the entire tree, but not over power or hide too much of the roots.

c)

After you are satisfied with the way the roots and root mound look, remove the tree and its base from the tray.

d)

You are now ready to decide whether you want to leave the root mound as a natural sand mound, or if you would prefer to have the sand look as if it has moss growing out of it. If you wish to leave the mound natural, skip the next step. (Adding color to your root mound).

14. ADDING COLOR TO THE ROOT MOUND

a)

To add color to the root mound that will appear to look like moss, you will need yellow, green, and white India Ink. Through trial and error, I have found that India Ink is the best medium to use on the sand. This ink will soak into the sand and it will keep its bright color for years, even if you place your tree in direct sunlight. This ink is also very opaque and the colors will not run into each other. India ink will not come out in the wash, so don't get it on clothing. Please do not use water color, acrylic, or oil paints for the root mound, I have tried them all and they just don't work for this application. You can buy India Ink at any store that sells art or craft supplies. You will need very little ink per tree, so buy the smallest bottle they offer. You will also need a small soft inexpensive artists or crafters brush. A size "1" or a "0" will do fine.

b)

Before you start the painting of the root mound, carefully bend all the branches of the tree straight up. This will keep them out of your way while you are painting.

c)

Starting with the green India Ink and the small soft brush, apply the ink to the root mound. The sand in the mound will actually draw the ink out of the brush so don't try to "paint" the sand. Let the ink be absorbed into the sand. Do not try to cover every grain of sand with the green ink. Allow some of the sand to remain in its natural color. I try to keep about 10% of the sand with no color on it at all. Try not to get any ink on the wire roots or trunk, this will not look natural, and you will need to scrape it off. If your sand is a mixture and contains any little pebbles, shells or pieces of wood or glass, try to also keep them un-painted and natural. This contrast in color and texture will make the root mound appear more realistic and give it much more depth. Proceed slowly, once the ink is on, there is no way to get it off! When you finish using your brush, wash it in warm water and a little soap or brush cleaner. Let it dry before you go on to the next color.

d)
After the green ink and your brush is dry, usually about 3 hours, apply the yellow ink. Use the same method as you did with the green ink, but apply only about 1/4 the total amount of yellow as you did green. Once again try to keep some of the sand and the other natural elements unpainted.

e)
After the yellow is dry. Apply the white ink. The white ink is used only as a highlight so apply very very little. Apply the white in small dots using only the tip of the brush. Use only enough white to cover a total of about 2% or less of the total area. You will be amazed how bright and white this ink is, and how little you need to use to create effective highlights. When you have finished adding all the color to the root mound, just let it dry. When it is dry, it is finished. Do not add any other coating or protection to the root mound, it will just dull the colors and is not necessary.

15. CREATING THE STYLE OF
TREE YOU WANT

Your tree is now ready for the final steps. Using the basic tree shape you just created you can form the trunk, branches and twigs into any of the following tree styles.

The Weeping Willow, The Wind Swept, The Oak.

a)
The Weeping Willow. This is the easiest of the three trees to form and requires very little cutting and shaping of the branches and twigs.

b)
The Wind Swept. To create the wind swept tree you will need to re-shape the trunk and trim some of the branches and twigs that appear to be too

long. This is not too difficult, and the effect is very dramatic. Of all the trees I create, the wind swept generates the most interest.

c)
The Oak. The oak is the most difficult of the three trees to create. It requires more twisting, bending and cutting of the branches and twigs. After you complete the oak, you will be able to create larger and more difficult tree sculpture.

If this is your first attempt at creating wire tree sculpture, I would suggest you start with the Weeping Willow. This is by far the easiest, and the results are satisfying.

16. CREATING THE WEEPING WILLOW

Of the three trees described in this book, the Weeping Willow is the easiest to create. This tree requires very little cutting and shaping and will give you a feel for working with the wire when you create other more complicated trees.

a)
Hold the tree firmly by the trunk. This is the best way to hold the tree securely while working on it. This grip will allow you to turn the tree and view if from different angles to be sure it is achieving the shape you want. b) Spread out all the branches so they look like a fan. All the branches should be on the same plane. This will make the tree appear flat, we will create roundness later on. *fig. 46.*

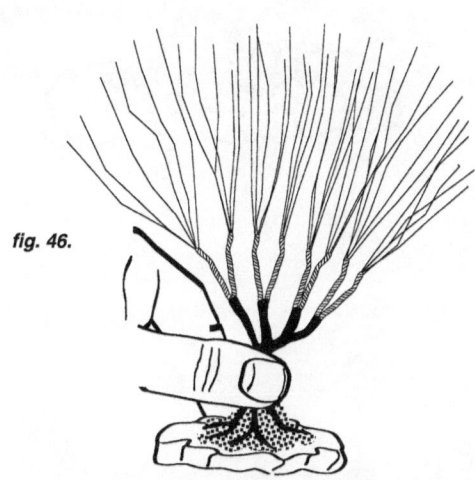

fig. 46.

c)

Hold the tree firmly at the top section of the trunk with one hand. With your other hand grip any 2 outermost branches at their "V" section, and twist the branches toward you 1/2 turn. *fig. 47.* This action will result in the 2 branches you have twisted becoming perpendicular to the branches next to them. Repeat this same function to every other set of 2 branches. The tree will now start to have a more rounded and full appearance.

fig. 47.

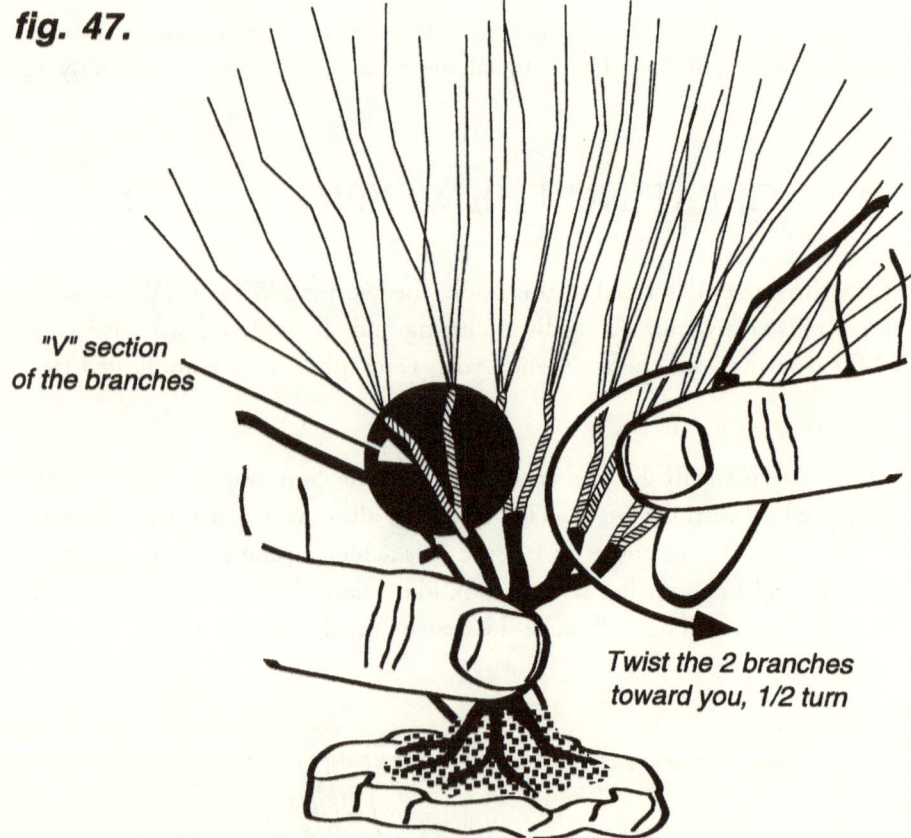

"V" section
of the branches

Twist the 2 branches
toward you, 1/2 turn

d)

Holding the tree at the point where the branches extend out of the trunk, place your index finger about half way up the branch. Start bending the wires over the roundness of your index finger so the ends of the branches point directly down. As you are bending the wires, try not to bend them all at the same point. Move your index finger to a point on the next branch that was different than the previous one. For more of a variety in the bending, bend the branch wires one at a time. *fg. 48.*

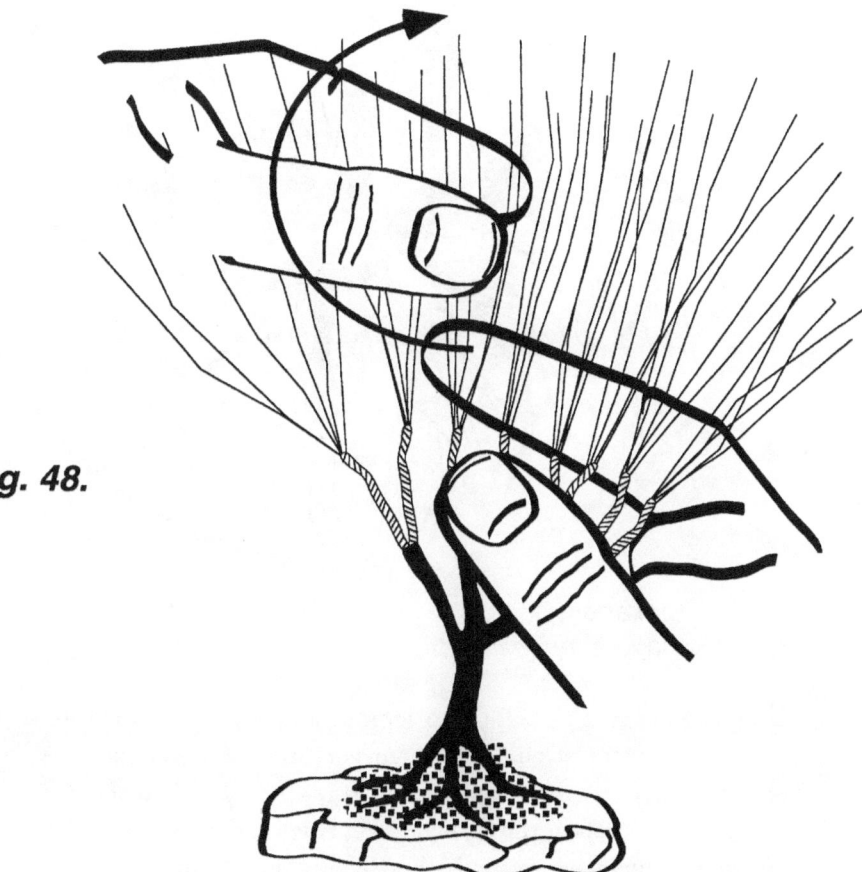

fig. 48.

e) As you are bending the branches, stop for a moment to look at the tree from directly above. *fig. 49.* The tree, when viewed from this angle, should have a round shape. If your tree looks flat, pull the branches away from each other to create the desired roundness.

fig.49.

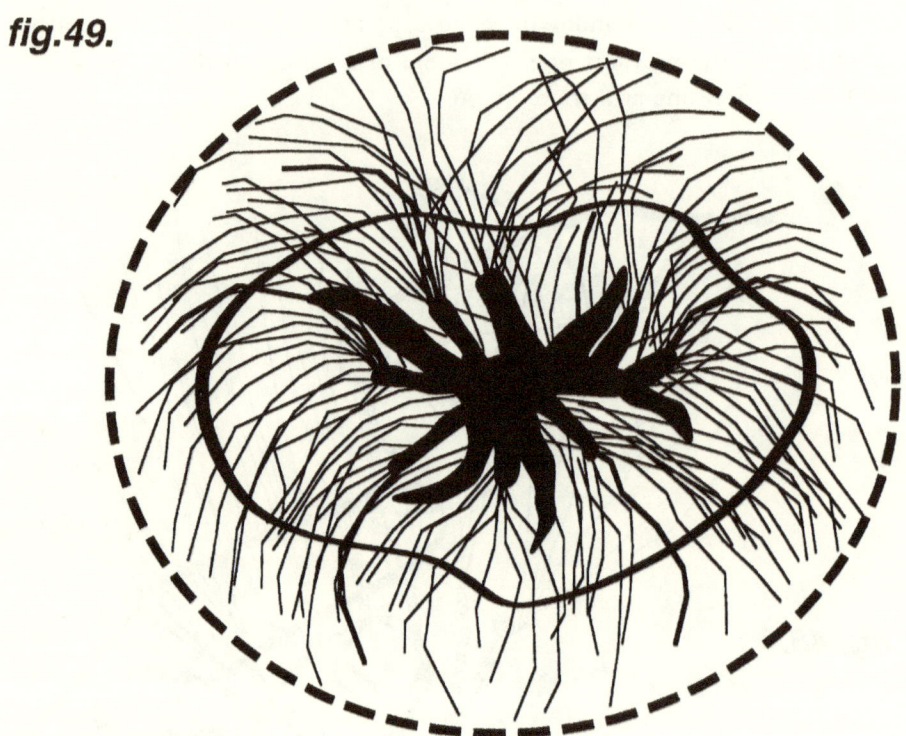

When viewed from above,
the tree should have a round like shape.

I have always found it very helpful to look at and study the structure of the trees. The variety is almost endless. When you are looking at the trees, note the relationship between the height of the trunk compared to the roots and the branches. Look closely at the branches and twigs and observe the interesting and sometimes strange shapes, twists and bends they form.

This is the final look of the Weeping Willow tree. If your tree does not appear as this one, or does not have the look you want, you can easily un-bend the wire branches and try again. Wire is very resilient and can be bent and unbent many times. You will find, as I did, that the more you work with the wire the better you get at it.

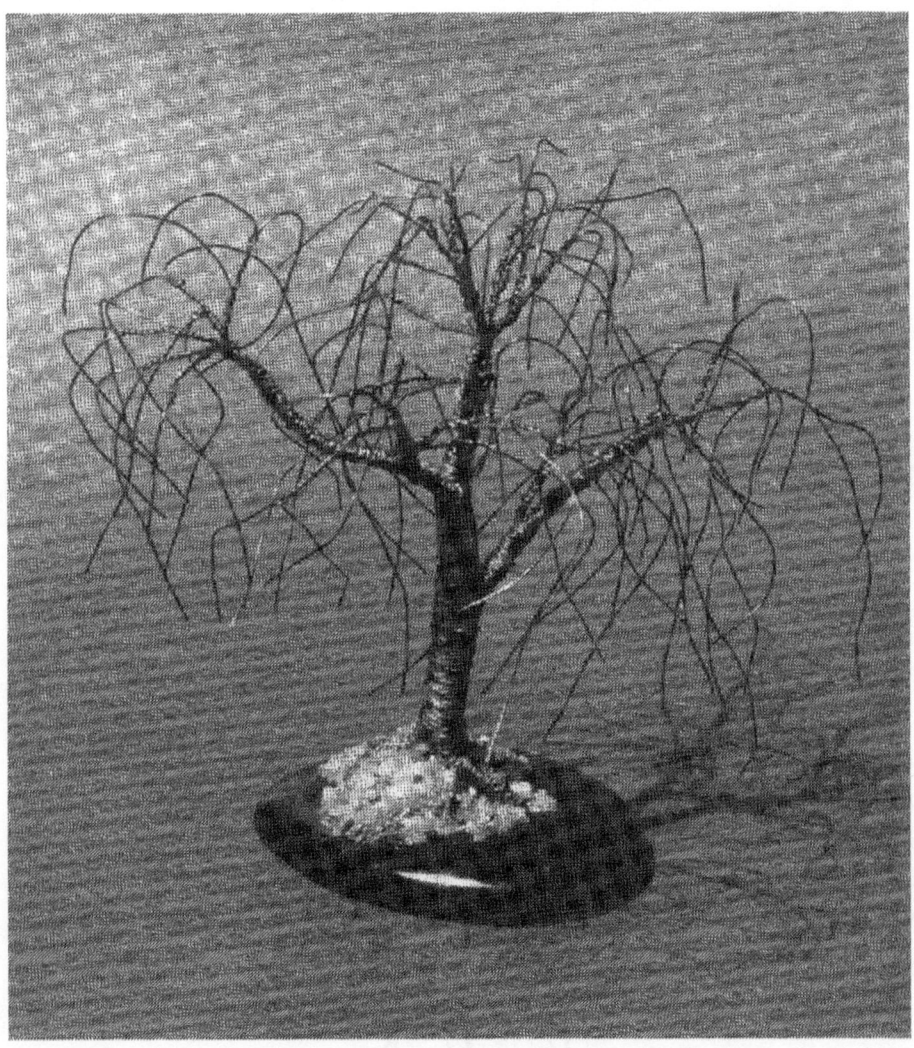

17. CREATING THE WIND SWEPT

Of all the trees I create, the Wind Swept receives the most interest. Perhaps people like the movement they see in it, or can relate to the tenacity of the tree holding fast against the force of a mighty wind.

a)
Hold the tree firmly by the trunk. This is the best way to hold the tree securely while working on it. This grip will allow you to turn the tree and view if from different angles to be sure it is achieving the shape you want.

b)
Spread out all the branches and twigs so they look like a fan. *fig. 50*. All the branches should be on the same plane. This will make the tree appear to be flat, however we will create its roundness later on.

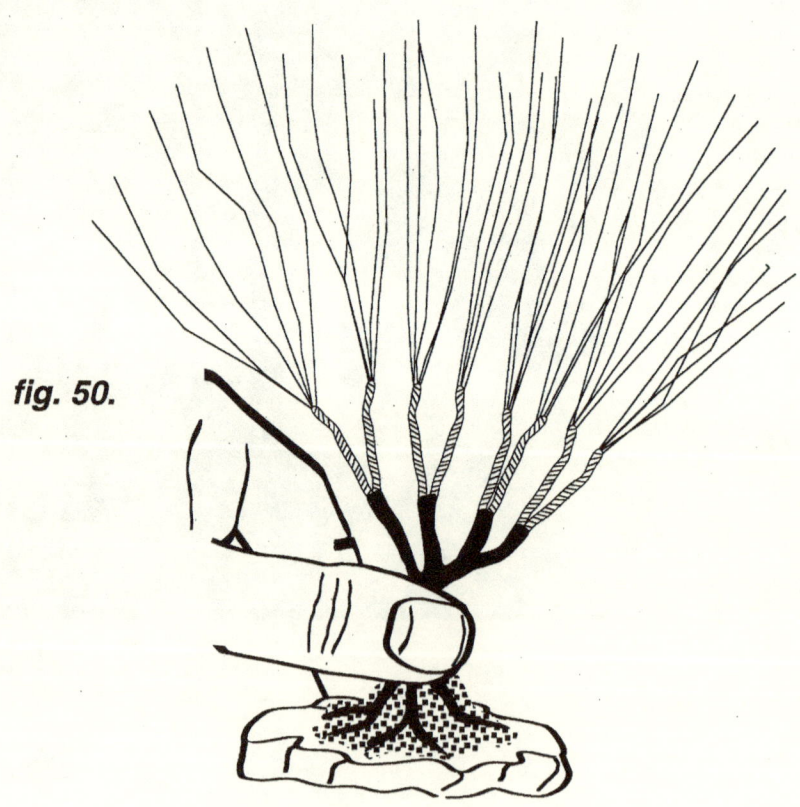

fig. 50.

c)

Hold the tree firmly at the top section of the trunk with one hand. With your other hand grip any 2 outermost branches at their "V" section, and twist the branches toward you 1/2 turn. *fig. 51*. This action will result in the 2 branches you have twisted becoming perpendicular to the branches next to them. Repeat this same function to every other set of 2 branches. The tree will now start to have a more rounded and full appearance.

fig. 51.

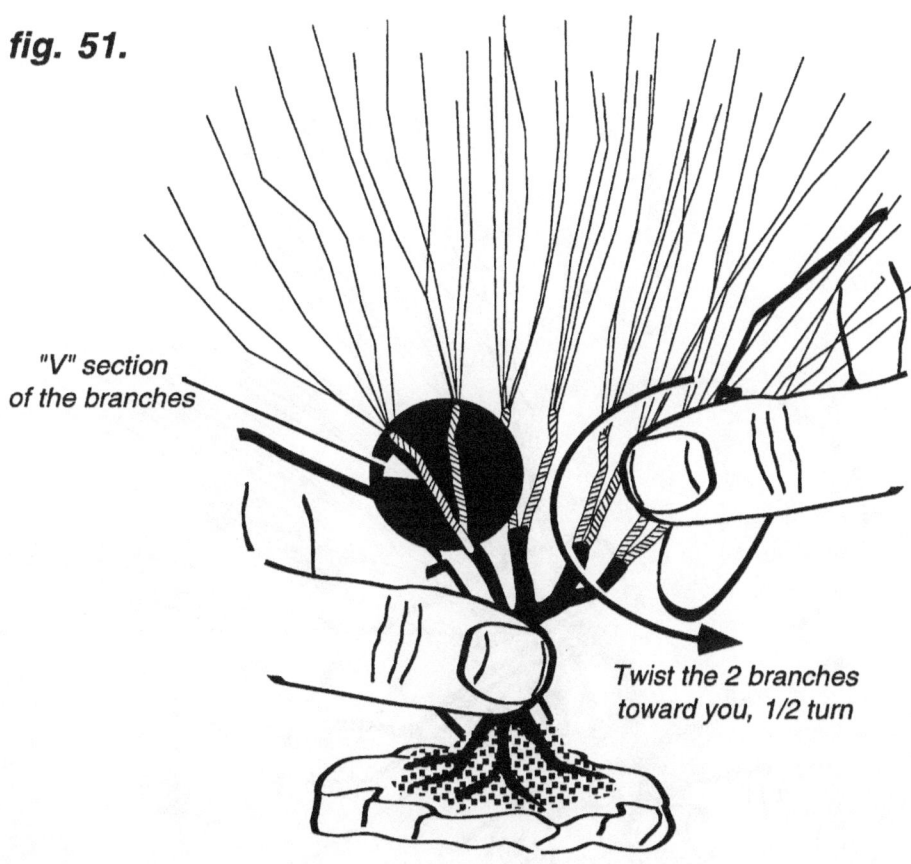

"V" section
of the branches

Twist the 2 branches
toward you, 1/2 turn

d)

You are now going to work on the trunk of the tree to give it the wind swept resistance look. Holding the tree at the base with one hand and place your thumb of the other hand about 1/2 way up the trunk. Slowly bend the entire trunk of the tree over your thumb as if you were trying to break the tree in half. Bend the trunk until the top of the trunk appears to be bent over about half way down the distance of a root. Don't worry about the wire snapping, it is very flexible and can be easily formed into this position. *fig. 52.*

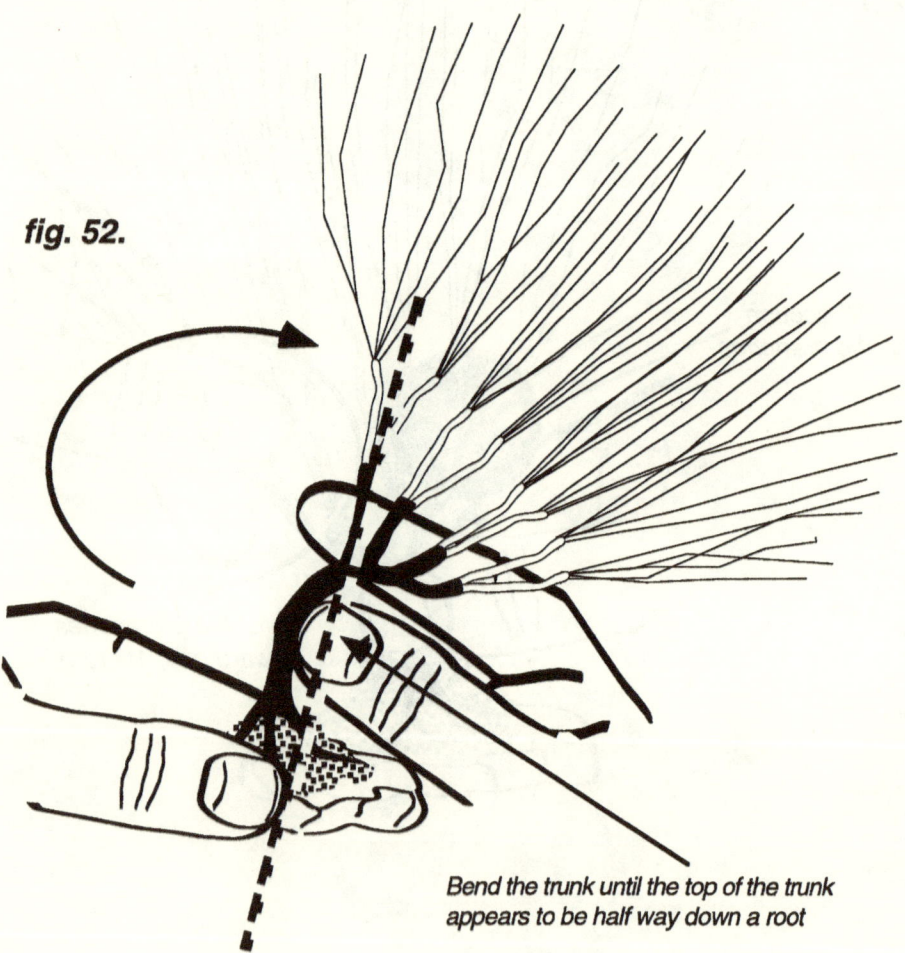

fig. 52.

Bend the trunk until the top of the trunk appears to be half way down a root

e)

Hold the tree firmly at the top of the trunk and bend a group of the branches in the opposite direction in which the trunk is bent. *fig. 53*. Do not try to bend too many branches at one time. This opposite bending is the action that will give the tree the appearance of bending, yet resisting, the force of the wind. As you bend the branches also separate any branches that appear to be too close together. Move some branches down and some up. For the most part the branches should all be basically parallel to each other, yet not exactly parallel. After all the bending is completed, if you feel any of the branches seem to be too long, cut them smaller using the small wire cutters.

fig. 53

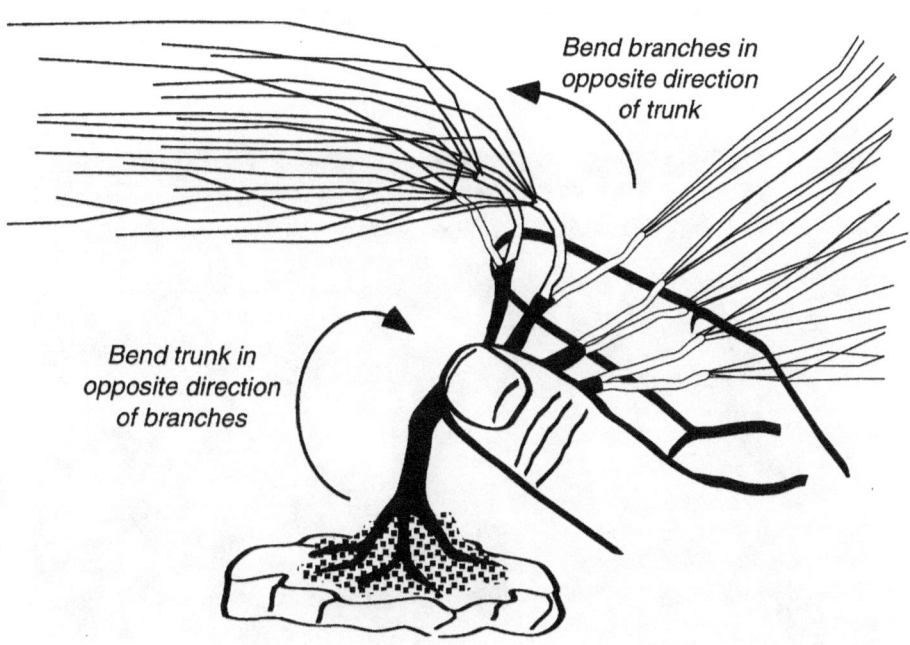

Bend branches in opposite direction of trunk

Bend trunk in opposite direction of branches

f)
As you are bending the branches, stop for a moment to look at the tree from directly above. *fig. 54.* The tree, when viewed from this angle, should have a oval and elongated shape. If your tree looks flat, pull the branches away from each other to create this shape

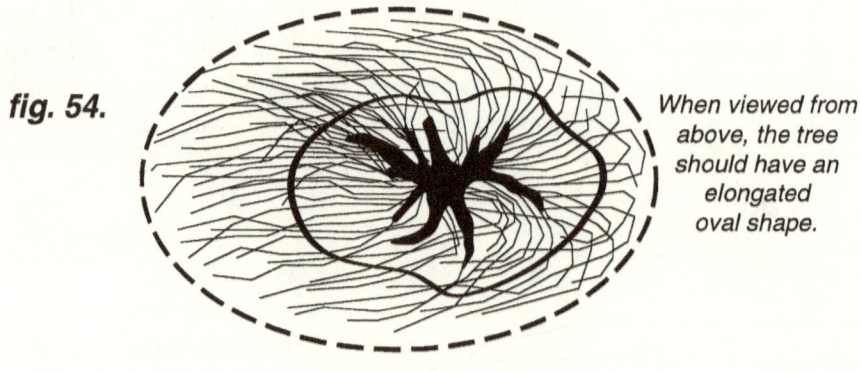

fig. 54.

When viewed from above, the tree should have an elongated oval shape.

The Wind Swept

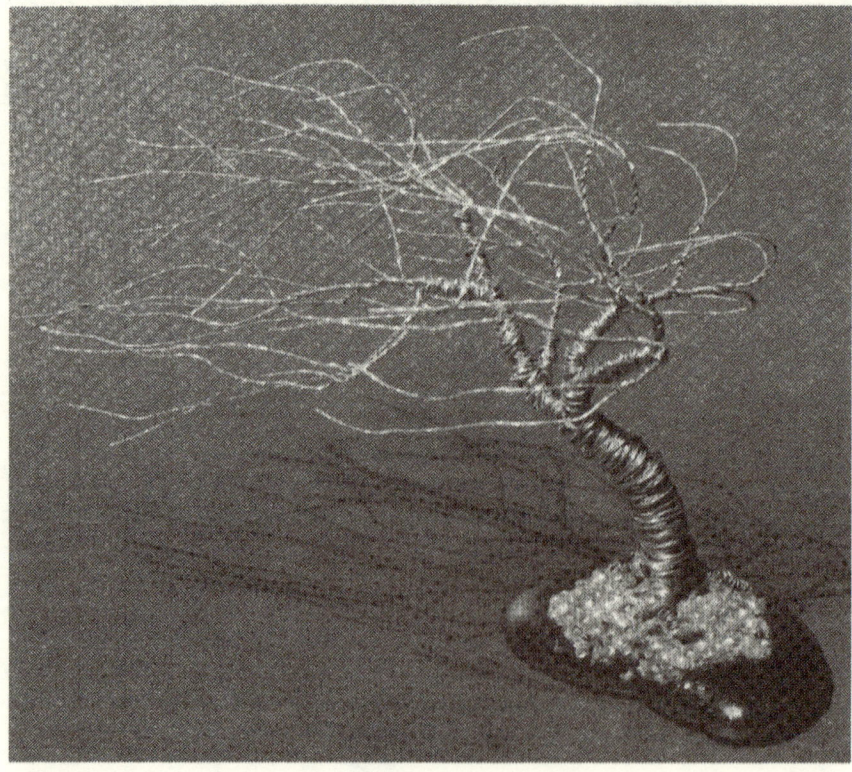

18. CREATING THE OAK TREE

The Oak tree is more difficult to create than the Weeping Willow or the Wind Swept. It will require more work on the branches and twigs. And will also involve some cutting of the longer twigs.

a) Hold the tree firmly by the trunk. This is the best way to hold the tree securely while working on it. This grip will allow you to turn the tree and view if from different angles to be sure it is achieving the shape you want.

b) Spread out all the branches and twigs so they look like a fan. All the branches should be on the same plane. This will make the tree appear to be flat, however we will create its roundness later on.

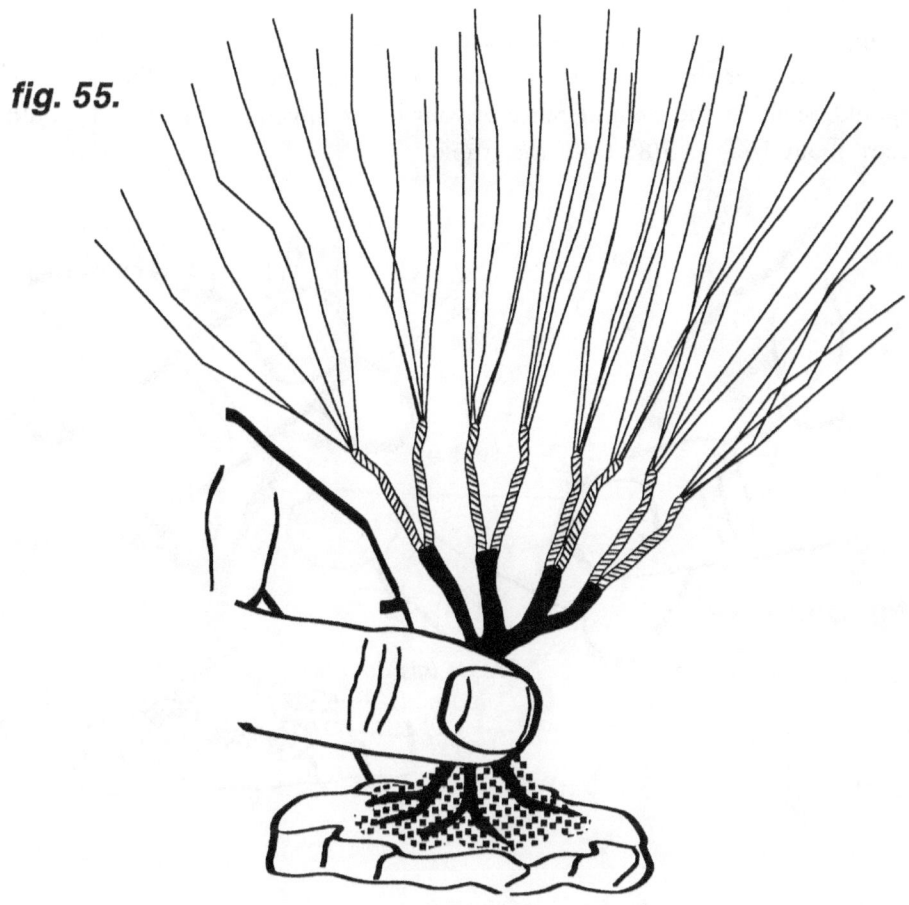

fig. 55.

c)

The following steps show how to create more and different size branches and twigs. The look of the Oak tree requires a more varied amount and size of branches and twigs. I think you will understand the procedures better if you read through all the steps before starting the Oak tree. In the following steps you will be cutting the wires to create the branches and twigs. So, it is important that you are sure of the procedure before you cut the wires. Remember, once you cut any of these branches, they will not grow back!

If you feel after reading all the following steps, you may have some difficulty making the branches and twigs, I would suggest using some scrap wire to practice with. Simply twist two pieces of the scrap wire to create a branch, then continue to follow the next steps.

d)

Gripping any outer branch at its base closest to the trunk of the tree, loop one single wire over the wire next to it and create an oval. *fig. 56*. The oval size should be about the circumference of your index finger. This first oval should start about 1/4" to 3/8" from the trunk.

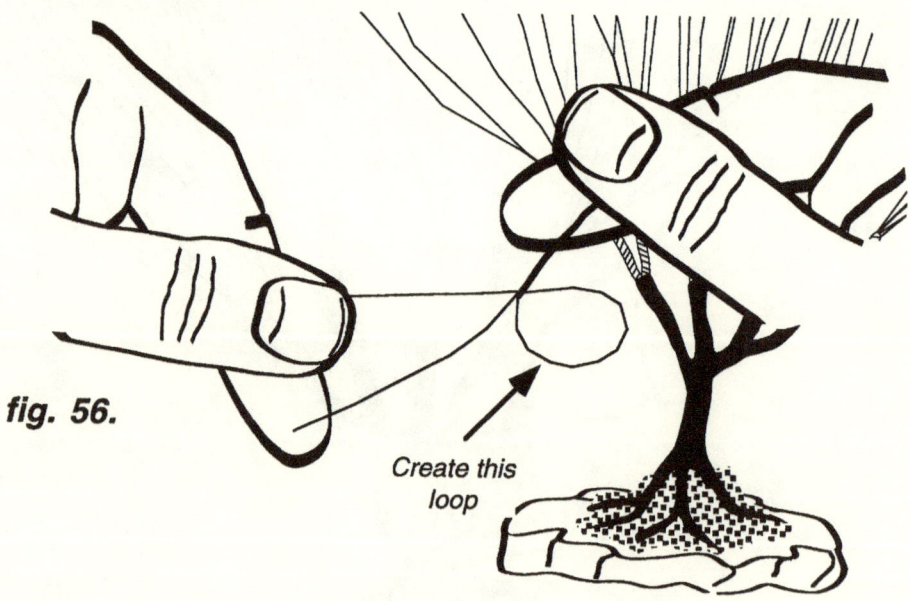

fig. 56.

Create this loop

e)

Hold the loop you just created and the other loose wires firmly and twist each in opposite directions about 4 or 5 twists. You can do each twist separately, holding one while you twist the other. *fig. 57.*

fig. 57.

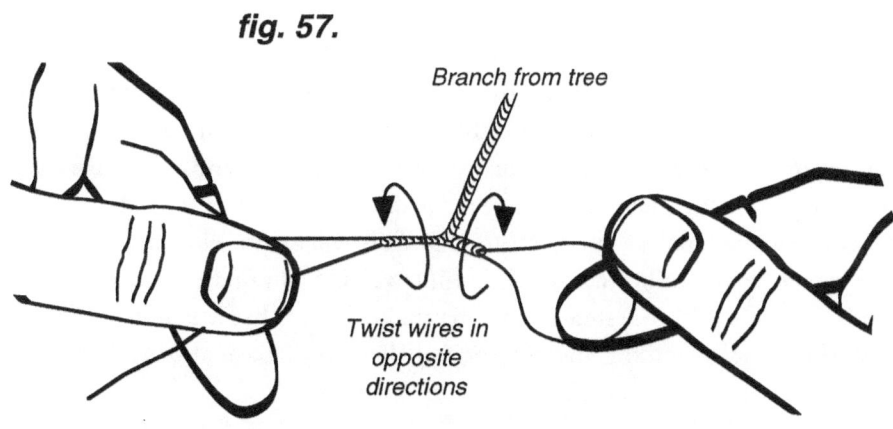

f)

Repeat step e), in each case using the longer of the two loose wires to create the next loop. Continue repeating step e), using the longer of the two loose wires to make the next loop. *fig. 58.* You should be able to create 2 to 4 loops per pair of wires. Do not be concerned if the loops are different sizes, this size difference will actually add more interest to the tree.

fig. 58.

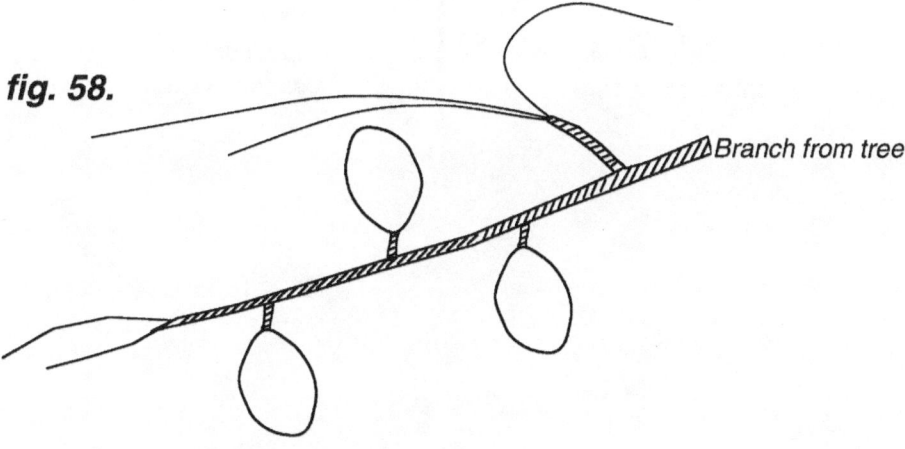

g)

Use the preceding steps on all the remaining pairs of wire branches on the tree. When you come across a branch with an extra wire that you cannot pair with another, just leave it as a single wire. All extra wires will be trimmed in the following steps.

h)

After you have created all the loops on the tree, you are now ready to cut the loops to create the final twigs. Use the small wire cutters for this step. I have learned through experience, and many tiny cuts in my hands, the safest way to cut the wire. Whenever you make a cut in the wire, try to keep the angle of the cut perpendicular to the wire. *fig. 59.* This will create blunter ends in the wire rather than "knife blades". This hint will not eliminate all cuts in your hands, but will help to lessen them. I have also found that it is much better to work slow when handling the cut ends of the wire. I have also tried working with gloves on, but I find the gloves too restricting.

fig. 59.

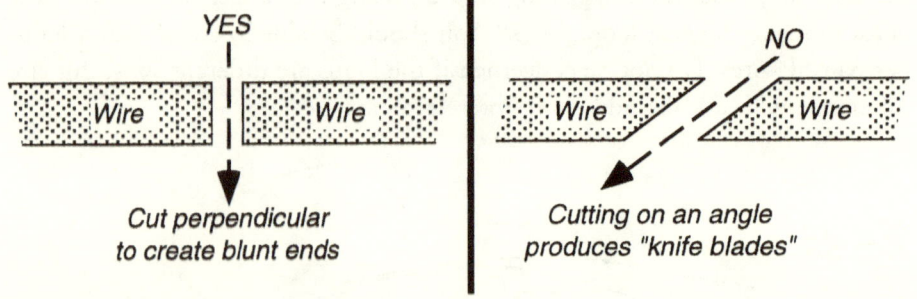

i)

Cut each loop once. This will create 2 twigs emanating from a larger branch. Do not cut the loops exactly in the center. Cut each loop in a different location to create twigs that are of different sizes. Hold each twig at the end and gently pull it to straighten it. The aim here is to take all of the circular shape out of the twig and make in more angular. If any of the end wires appear too long, now is the time to trim them. *fig. 60.*

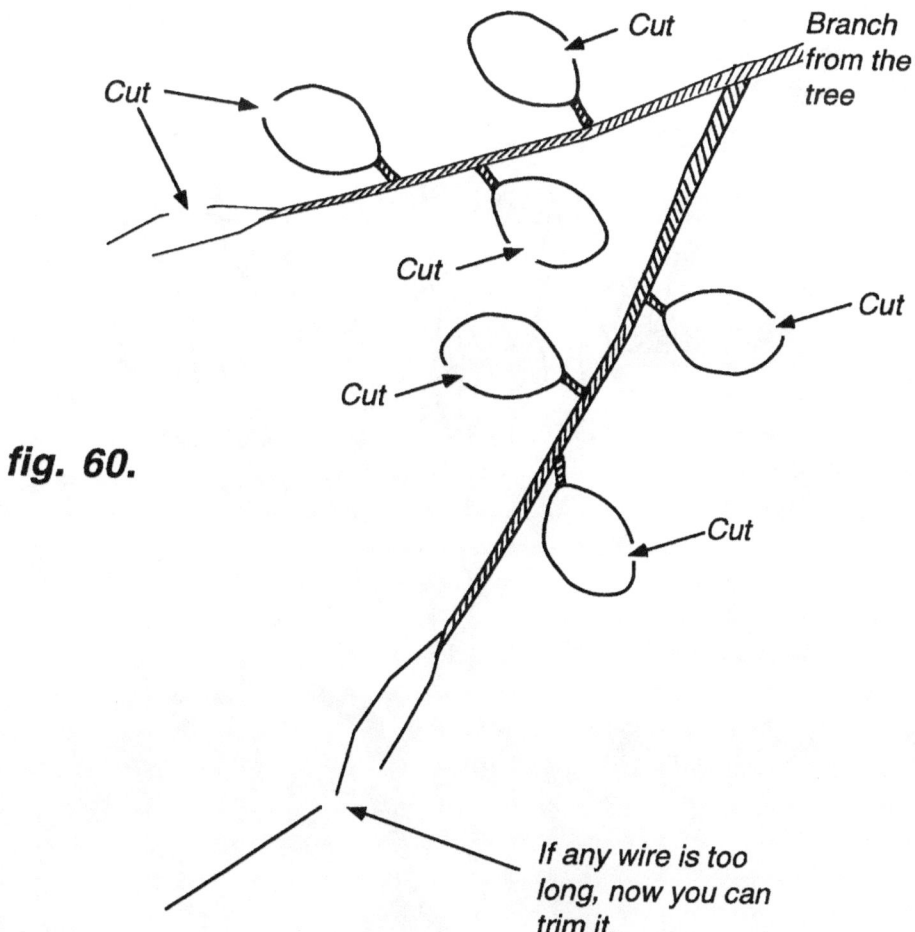

fig. 60.

j)
We are now at the point where you will make all that wire actually look like
an Oak tree. This is perhaps the most artistically difficult part, but it is also
the most rewarding. If, after you complete the following steps, you do not
like the look of your tree, you can very easily repeat these final steps. The wire
is very workable and can be bent and reshaped many times before it breaks.
fig. 61.

k)
Push all the branches and twigs straight up, and flatten the sections of the
branches that are closest to the top of the trunk. Spread out and separate the
main branches.

fig. 61.

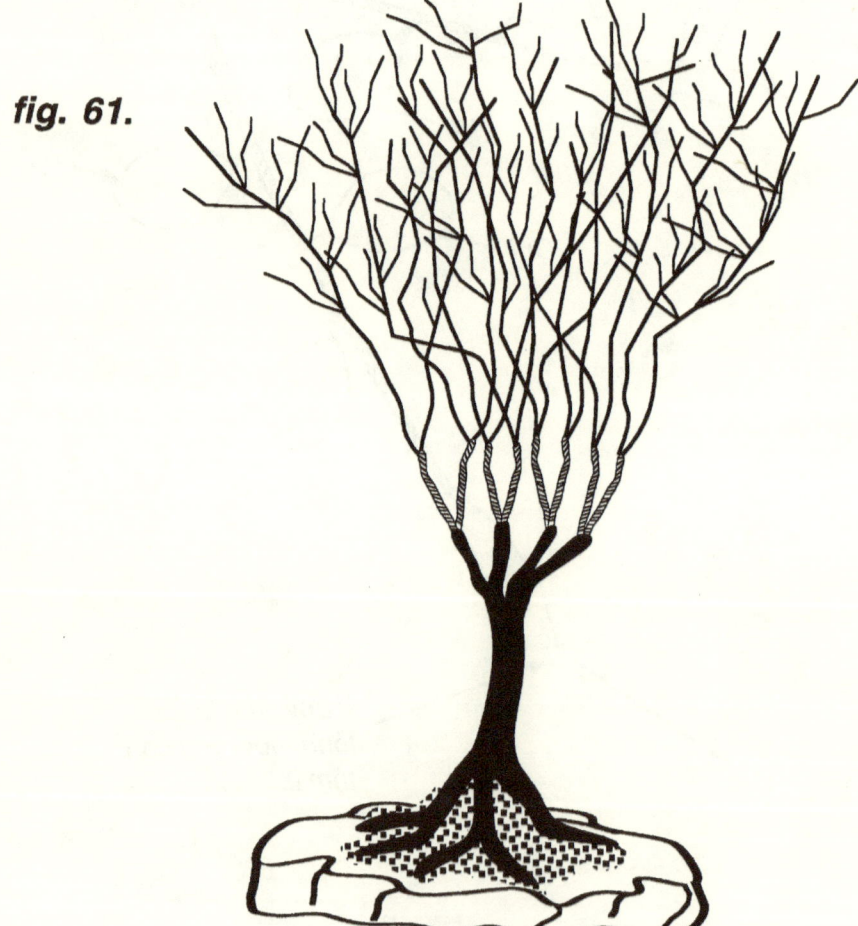

l)

You are now going to begin to style and shape the outermost twigs of the tree. *fig. 62.* If you have ever looked closely at the twigs of an Oak tree, (or almost any tree) you may have noticed that the twigs seem to go in every conceivable direction with no particular rhyme or reason. They are not equally spaced apart, nor are they all bunched together. I have been told that this is due to the efforts of the tree to receive as much sunlight as possible by twisting each leaf into the direction of the sun. This is more noticeable in the winter, when there are no leaves to obstruct your view.

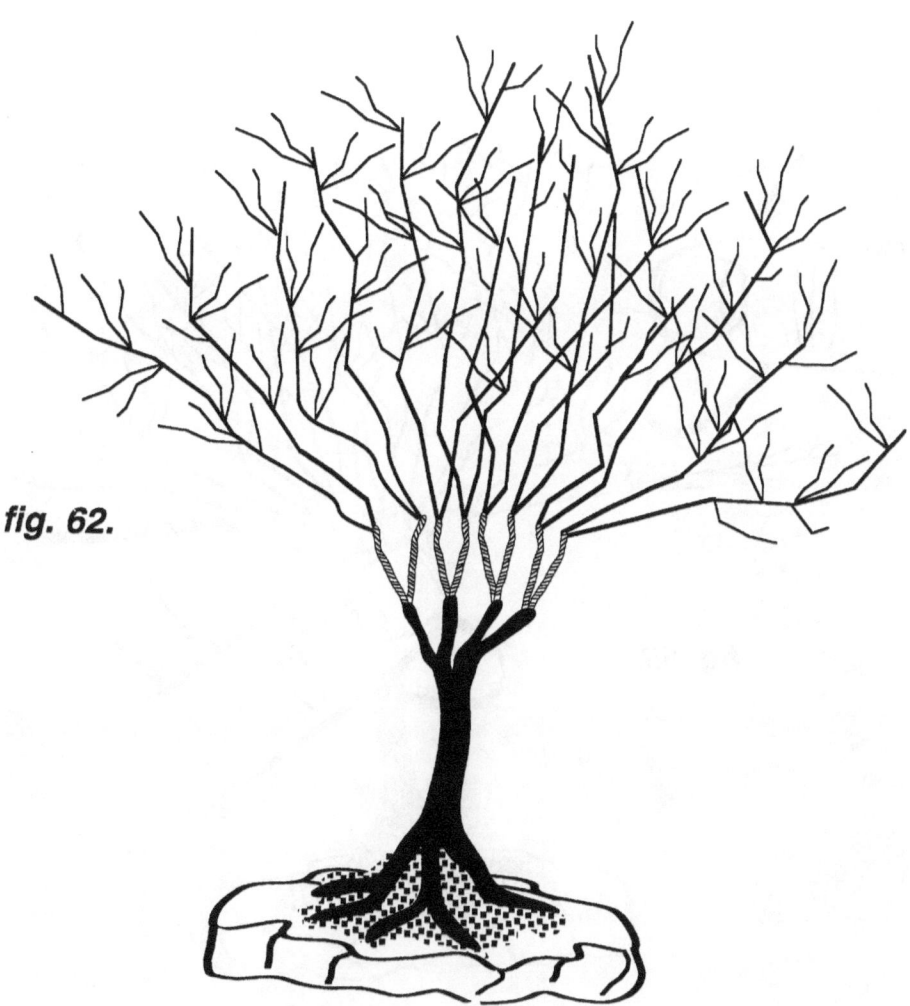

fig. 62.

The structure of wire you are using lends itself very nicely to capturing the randomness of the twigs. Keeping the reason and the structure of the twigs in mind as you work, fan out all twigs so that no two twigs are touching. After this is completed your tree should look like an opened fan.

m)
Hold the tree from the top section of the trunk and bend each of the branches in the opposite direction of the branch next to it. This action will start to give the tree a more rounded and full look. *fig. 63.*

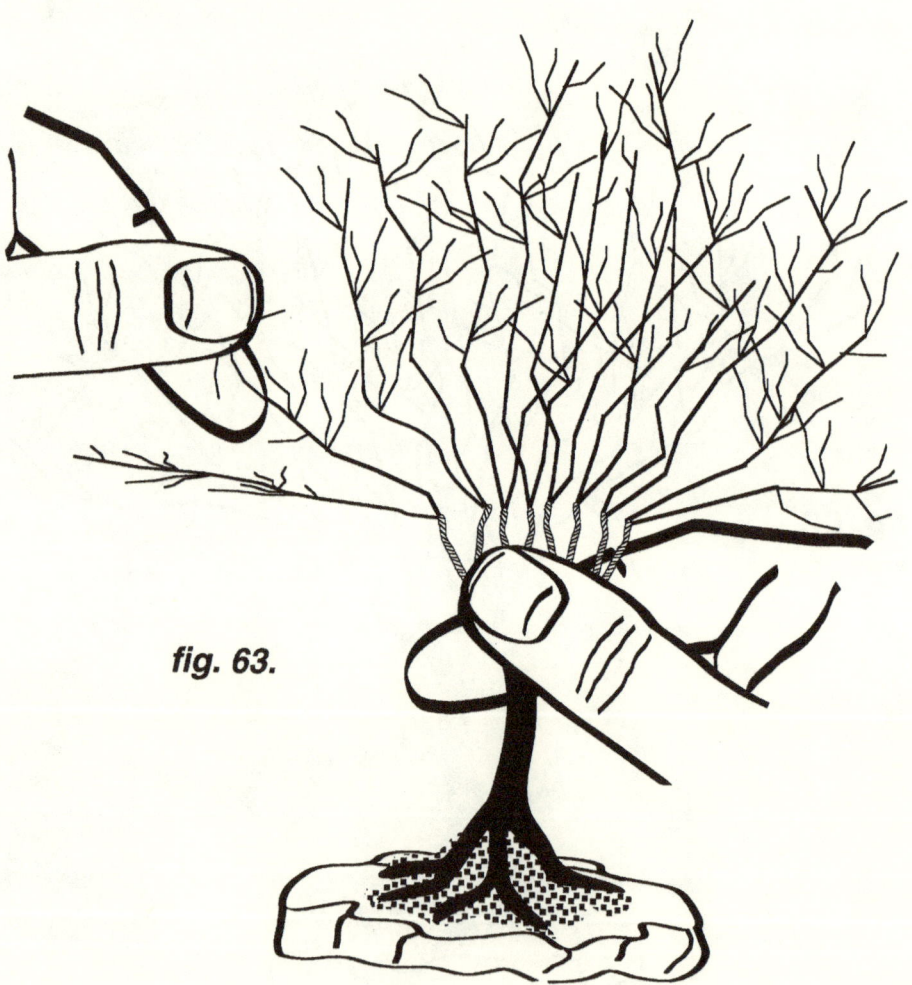

fig. 63.

n)

As you are bending the twigs, stop for a moment to look at the tree from directly above. *fig. 64*. The tree, when viewed from this angle, should have a round shape. If your tree looks flat, pull the branches away from each other to create the necessary roundness.

fig. 64.

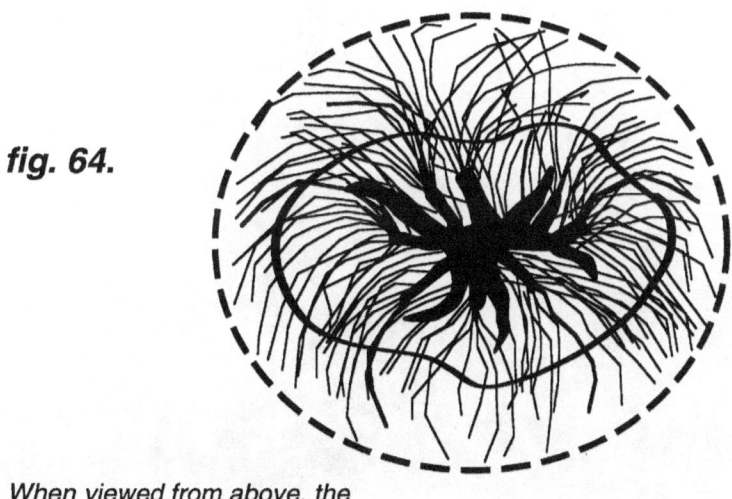

When viewed from above, the tree should have a round shape.

o)

As a final bending step to create more variety in the shape of the twigs, bend about every third twig at a 90 degree angle at the half way point on the twig. *fig. 65*.

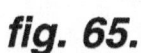

fig. 65.

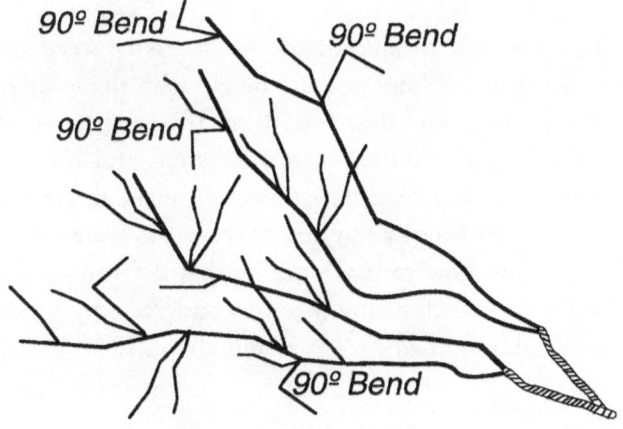

The Oak Tree

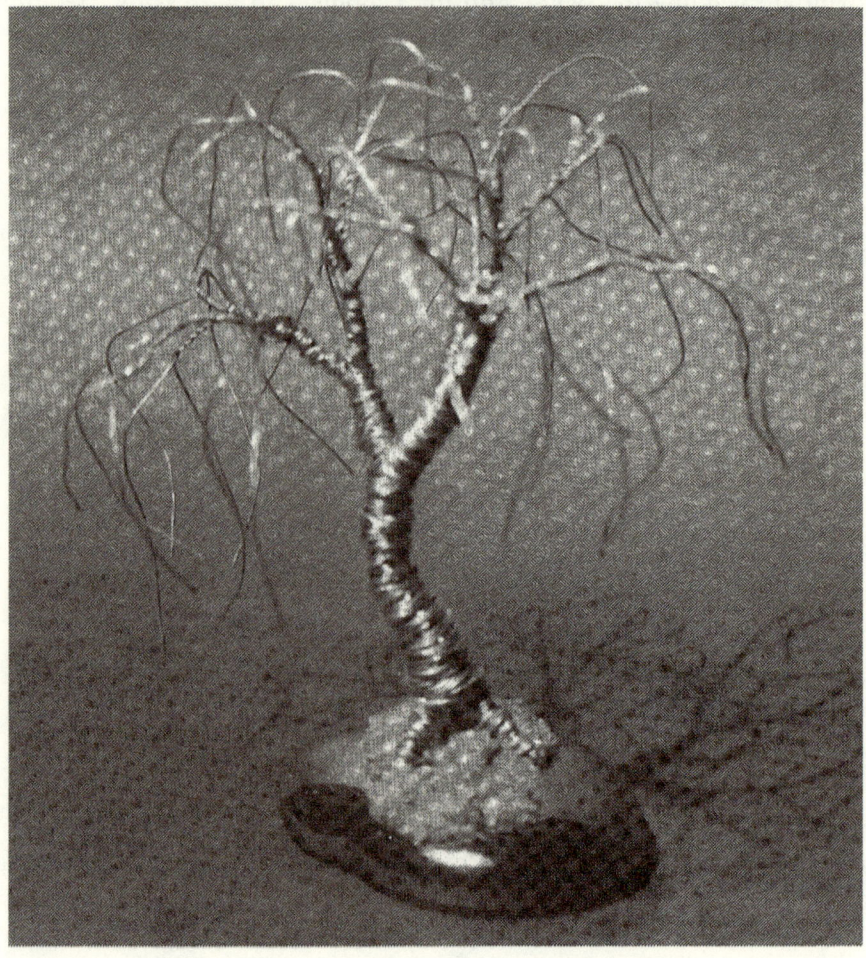

You have now completed all the necessary steps and procedures to create a tree sculpture. I hope you are happy with the results. I have tried to make the steps as simple and clear as possible. If you wish to create other trees of different size and shape you can use these steps and tools as your guide. I strongly suggest that you try different ways to make the tree sculptures, and also try to use different gauge and types of wire. You were shown at the beginning of the instructions how to make the jig that determines the amount of wire needed for the tree. And, you may have wondered why I didn't instruct you to simply cut X amount of wire to a set amount, and start to wrap. Once you understand what the jig is for, and used it, you will be able to alter the position of the nails and increase the number of wraps and create other trees of different size and shapes.

You may have also noticed that I did not tell you how long it should take you to make your tree sculpture. I don't think it is of any value to place a time frame on yourself when creating. People sometimes ask me "how long did it take you to create that tree?" (usually they are asking about a large tree that took many many hours), my standard answer is . . . it took me 25 years to learn, and 25 hours to create! Creating art is the process that took you to the point at which you now find yourself. It is never finished. Every time someone asks me how long my art takes to create, I say to myself, what an unimportant question. What difference does it make how long a piece of art took to create? The result is what matters. The beauty is in the piece, not the time! However, whenever someone asks me how do you make those trees, I know I am talking with an art lover!

If you would like to see more of my tree sculptures please visit my web site, and once again, I hope you are happy with your tree sculpture.

I would be happy to hear from you with any comments or suggestions. You can contact me at:

Sal Villano—P.O. Box 514, Miller Place, NY 11764
Studio Phone & Fax: 631-928-2644
email: salvillano@gmail.com
Web Site: www.salvillano.com

ABOUT THE ARTIST

Sal Villano was born in New York City in 1944 into a large extended family of artists. From a very young age he was aware of art in his life and attracted to visual expression. Sal attended public grade school, high school and graduated college with a degree in commercial art. In addition, he continued to pursue his love of art at the Art Students' League in Manhattan. While still in college, Sal worked part time with his uncle, Charles Santaniello, a sculptor who created magnificent displays for commercial accounts and several World Fairs. It was during this collaboration with his uncle that Sal realized he too wanted to be a sculptor.

After graduating college, Sal began his career as a commercial artist, working in Manhattan. In 1969, Sal established his own art studio with another artist. This partnership lasted for a long period of time and provided Sal the opportunity to explore a wide variety of commercial work. Commissioned by several large national and international companies, Sal, along with his partner, produced a large variety of two and three dimensional work.

It was during his studies at the Art Students' League that Sal created his first wire tree sculpture. While constructing a wire armature to support a clay figure, Sal observed that the wire he was using could be bent, twisted and wrapped to look like a tree! Since that day, so many years ago, Sal has created hundreds of tree sculptures, in sizes from two inches and up, using a large variety of wire types, colors, and gauges. Each sculpture is carefully incorporated with a base which is a vital visual addition to the art work.

Each sculpture is a unique work, and, as in nature, no two trees can ever be created alike.

HOW TO CREATE
Tree Sculpture
By Sal Villano

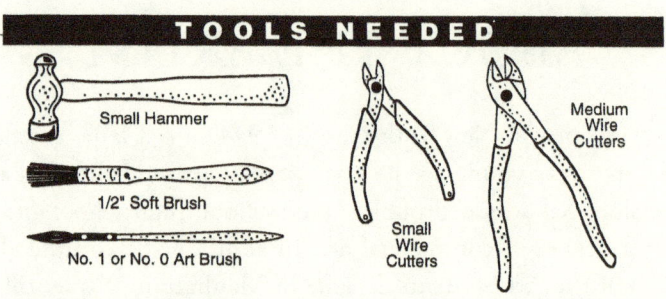

TOOLS NEEDED

Small Hammer

1/2" Soft Brush

No. 1 or No. 0 Art Brush

Small Wire Cutters

Medium Wire Cutters

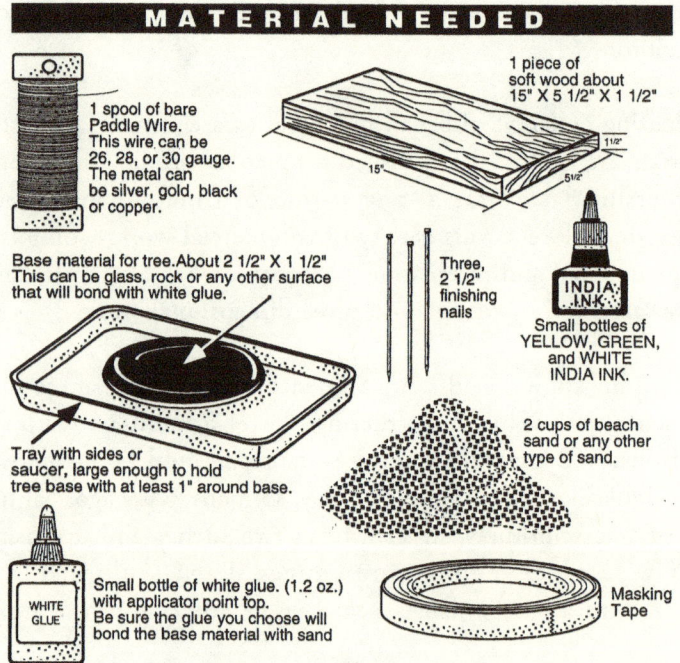

MATERIAL NEEDED

1 spool of bare Paddle Wire. This wire can be 26, 28, or 30 gauge. The metal can be silver, gold, black or copper.

1 piece of soft wood about 15" X 5 1/2" X 1 1/2"

Base material for tree. About 2 1/2" X 1 1/2" This can be glass, rock or any other surface that will bond with white glue.

Three, 2 1/2" finishing nails

Small bottles of YELLOW, GREEN, and WHITE INDIA INK.

Tray with sides or saucer, large enough to hold tree base with at least 1" around base.

2 cups of beach sand or any other type of sand.

Small bottle of white glue. (1.2 oz.) with applicator point top. Be sure the glue you choose will bond the base material with sand

WHITE GLUE

Masking Tape

Sal Villano—P.O. Box 514, Miller Place, NY 11764
Studio Phone & Fax: 631-928-2644
email: salvillano@gmail.com
Web Site: www.salvillano.com

www.ingramcontent.com/pod-product-compliance
Lightning Source LLC
Chambersburg PA
CBHW021904170526
45157CB00005B/1967